The Aviatrix

Fly Like a Girl

by Kimberley Jochl

Wilfred Lee Books
Village of Sugar Mountain, North Carolina
www.kimberleyjochl.com

ISBN 978-0-9971507-0-4

Cover and interior designs: Diana Wade dwadegraphics.com

Cover photography: Todd Bush www.bushphoto.com

Table of Contents

For those who took the time to teach me

Introduction

Ever since I was a little girl, being afraid was really never my problem. Timid and thoughtful was more like it. But then I grew up, and slowly but surely, flying with my experienced pilot husband in our Piper Cheyenne became problematic. Well, more than problematic. It scared me to death. So I earned my private pilot's license.

Every simple task, each minor step, and every accomplishment was an emotional, psychological, and physical milestone. Neither fear nor my discouraging inner voice nor the elements of Mother Nature could distract me from becoming a pilot. I found security in my flight instructor, encouragement and confidence from my husband, an available ear from my twin sister, and rewarded myself with the pleasures of french fries, a Coke, and a cheeseburger from McDonald's after many training sessions. Feeling like a Bond girl every now and then was hair-raising.

The process was all-consuming, every day. Seven months after my nutty idea evolved into an obsession, I became an official private pilot, and shortly thereafter, the owner of a 1969 Cessna Skylane. Being a female pilot with a red single-engine airplane had lots of advantages most of the time. For instance I could travel anytime and pretty much anywhere. Airport personnel were impressed with my vintage model aircraft. And the fact that I was a girl often got me speedy and friendly service. My parents didn't really believe it, my older sister was scared, and some of my friends were stunned. My husband convinced me that working alongside him on the Skylane's overhaul, the constant upkeep, and maintenance would be rewarding and educational. It was.

The Aviatrix is a candid, sometimes funny, definitely scary but straightforward, behind-the-scenes, firsthand look into the process of becoming a pilot. I tell you what most pilots, especially men, won't dare whisper. I explain terms, concepts, and procedures in a way that even a blonde could grasp. And I think when you're finished reading my book you'll feel as though you can do something you never thought you could. Just like me.

CHAPTER ONE
Deathly Afraid

I was afraid, deathly afraid, of flying. No joke, I thought I was going to have a heart attack whenever I flew in a small airplane. I did everything to slow my heartbeat to a manageable rate. My hands shook. I broke out in a sweat; my muscles became weak and lethargic. Sometimes I thought my only relief would be to pass out.

So I earned my private pilot's license.

My husband, Gunther, has been a pilot for over thirty years and loves it. *Really* loves it. It's his relief, his joy, his passion. The challenge and the freedom of flying fills a space in his soul that nothing else can. We have an airplane, a Piper Cheyenne II. It's a twin-engine turbo-prop; it seats eight, cruises at 260 knots, has a range of about 1,200 nautical miles, and even has a toilet. It's a wonderful luxury, the airplane (and that toilet!). Gunther flew the Cheyenne from Banner Elk, North Carolina, to Straubing, Germany, in 1989 with his best friend, Dick, a retired two-star general in the Marine Corps. Not only does Gunther hold a commercial, multi-engine, instrument flight rules (IFR) rating pilot's license, but he's also a certified Federal Aviation Administration airframe and power plant mechanic (FAA A&P).

Gunther's a German-educated mechanical engineer, so for him, *working* on airplanes is also a stress reliever, a joy, and a passion. Much of his leisure and therapy time is spent with the

Cheyenne. We've flown to many, many places in the past, and naturally he intends to fly forever.

It was clear: there was just no room in our life for me to be fearful of flying.

Flying commercially was never a problem for me. As a matter of fact, I enjoyed it and found it relaxing except for those rare and random incidents that cause every airline passenger to hold their breath and hope for the best—like when the airplane is about to touch down and without warning the nose pitches up, the engines rev into overdrive, and you're climbing rapidly back into the sky. As the airplane approaches safety the pilot comes over the loudspeaker to inform the petrified load of passengers that everything is okay, just another airplane on the runway forcing us to abort the landing. Most of us get over those types of incidents and hop effortlessly back on the next flight.

Since we owned an airplane and flew privately, I had been encouraged by lots of friends and family over the years to get a pilot's license. "You know, Kim, if anything ever happens to Gunther while you two are flying, you should know what to do. At least know how to land the airplane," they gently scolded. But I never, ever had the desire to learn how to fly. I reasoned that Gunther's a strong, determined, healthy man—not to mention an accomplished and experienced pilot. I could never take on the enormous responsibility of piloting an airplane. Smart, disciplined, and confident people fly airplanes. There's a special kind of person who innately believes that she can control such a large piece of machinery safely, in all of Mother Nature's powerful elements; I just wasn't that person. Being a passenger was always just fine with me—until I became fearful of flying.

Suddenly, I didn't even want to be a passenger anymore. Maybe it was my age, raising a family or that subconscious fear that perhaps something may happen to Gunther at 27,000 feet (then what?) that brought on a new, unreasonable fear in me. Regardless, it was a problem.

Gunther was always very understanding and generously sympathetic of my fears when we flew. He'd often suggest that I sit "right seat" (that's the copilot's position) so I could understand what was going on, or if I was in the back, he'd keep me posted throughout the flight. It helped a little, but I was still petrified.

I yearned for a solution, and wouldn't you know it—the impossible appeared. This sounds crazy, but one random day in early May I looked into the sky and saw a small airplane serenely crossing the horizon. *I can do that,* I said to myself. *I can fly an airplane.* Right then and there I decided I was going to learn how to fly. It must have been divine intervention, truly, because I would never have made this decision on my own.

The small airport in Elizabethton, Tennessee, forty-five minutes from my home, has a great teaching reputation among the local flying community. I called the Elizabethton Municipal Airport and asked about the flight-training program. I spoke with Dan, the airport manager, who offered a brief background about the flight instructors.

Within a few hours, John, who became my flight instructor, called me on my cell. I was at work. *So quickly?* I thought. I was overtaken with panic. *This isn't real.*

We scheduled an introductory flight for Saturday, May 18, my forty-third birthday.

I arrived on time and John was there waiting. As we shook hands, I was struck by his calm and comforting demeanor. I thought, *This guy's waaaay too calm for me. I'll never be able to slow down to his pace.* Work, family, and just plain old life have evolved me into a fast-paced, busy kind of girl. John and I walked to the ground instruction room, sat down at the worktable, and talked briefly. He told me a little bit about his credentials as a flight instructor. I have no idea what I told him, except that I was afraid to fly.

Okaaaay, I wonder how long this will last? John must have thought.

"Let's go take a look at the airplane," he said, seeming to ignore my fear while making my desire to fly the priority.

"Okay," I said with scared excitement. John walked slowly and methodically to the spotless, sterile hangar that housed three adorable airplanes. I walked timidly next to him.

There it is: a death trap, I thought.

It was a blue-and-black-on-white Cessna Skyhawk 172 single-engine.

"Go on in," he said.

"In the pilot's seat?" I questioned.

"Yes," he said easily. I soon came to realize John's pace and demeanor were exactly what I needed to get me in the air and flying.

That first day, though, it was raining, so we couldn't fly; this was the only reason I could disguise my extreme emotions. I just followed directions, quiet as could be, definitely beside myself. I sat in the pilot's seat. John got in the copilot's seat. I was in awe of the enormous and incomprehensible task that lay ahead and thought, *We are both crazy to even consider me flying this machine!* But I was also excited. I looked at the instrument panel, fixing my eyes on each instrument, one by one. I didn't have any clue what I was looking at. Well, that's not entirely true; I knew some basics from flying in the Cheyenne. But knowing about something didn't mean I could properly apply the knowledge. Regardless, I was on my way.

Three days later, I was in the left seat of the Skyhawk. John was in the right seat and doing all the flying. I did have my hands and feet on the flight controls, but I didn't dare apply any pressure or make any moves short of breathing, in fear of inadvertently causing the airplane to suddenly plummet from the sky.

It was a bumpy day, and John didn't explain that there was no need to worry—and boy, was I worried. With every bump I held my breath and even let out a few oh nos. Okay, every bump I said out loud, "Oh no!" John was probably thinking *Either this'll be a short summer for her, or a long summer for me.* I got through the flight—more frightened than I had been before it. *One hour down, thirty-nine more to go.* For some reason, I had it in my head that after forty hours of flight training, I would be home free and I'd have my license. Little did I know that earning a private pilot's license requires a minimum forty hours of flying experience, twenty hours with a flight instructor, ten hours of solo flying, a medical exam, a written exam, an oral exam, and a practical exam—the latter two with an FAA examiner.

After my introductory flight lesson, I bought $320 worth of textbooks, an E6B (a basic, non-computerized aviation calculator that computes true airspeed, heading, wind correction angle, true temperature, nautical miles to statute miles, and so much more), and a plotter, which marks the course of the flight and measures distance on sectional charts. These are stone-age tools, but still useful. It seemed I was committed, financially anyway.

We scheduled another flight for May 23. In the meantime, I was reading my two-inch thick Jeppesen *Guided Flight Discovery Private Pilot* textbook. It was great reading. (I'm serious!) I found the content interesting, and eventually it became addicting. I loved reading it and completed every question at the end of every chapter. Gunther helped me quite a bit when I had questions, or couldn't quite grasp a concept.

Flying became the main topic at our dinner table, and any other time too. Olivia, our twelve-year-old daughter, was not interested. She often had to fight to get a word in during dinner conversations. Eventually her iPhone and iPad occupied her, rather than her parents' conversations.

During flight lessons, John suggested several times that I bring Olivia along. *That's a good idea!* I thought.

So I asked her, "Olivia, do you want to fly with me?"

"No," she said.

"Why not?"

"It's boring," she replied.

All right, fair enough, I thought.

But Krista, my identical twin sister, who lives in Washington, DC, was a different matter. She was all over it and couldn't wait to fly with me at the earliest opportunity. She's a daredevil. She even jumped out of a perfectly good airplane once. (I, on the other hand, wouldn't be caught dead jumping out of an airplane.)

Without warning one day Mom received a package in the mail from Krista containing a videotape and a note that said, *Watch.* Mom popped the tape in the VCR, turned the TV on, and took a seat. There was Krista, flying tandem through the air with her hand pasted up against the TV screen. On her hand printed with

a Sharpie it said, *Hey Mom. Crazy!* That's Krista. I'm the opposite.

I was apprehensive and not completely excited about Krista coming along on a flight with me. After all, I was still deathly afraid to fly, and any detour from the routine made me even more uptight. But I knew she would enjoy it. So I put my apprehension aside—but not without giving her strict instructions.

I never shy away from being bossy with Krista when necessary. "Krista, you are not allowed to ask any questions, don't talk too much, and if you take any pictures, they'd better not be posted on Facebook," I commanded.

"Okay, Kim," she replied. I knew better.

Krista is the more outgoing twin, and tends to walk with purpose into the spotlight. She talks more easily with strangers and loves to tell untrue stories about us. I, on the other hand, prefer to listen, feel people out. I'm guarded; she's not. I favor reality over stories.

On our first flight together, she behaved very well, mostly. As we entered the terminal prior to the flight, hung around her like a duffel bag was her high-tech, super-duper big camera.

I rolled my eyes and said, "I better not be on Facebook."

Of course, I was on Facebook, piloting the airplane—left seat at about 4,000 feet—within hours of the flight's completion. John was right seat and Krista was in the back taking the pictures.

Krista loved every minute of the flight. She was proud of her little sister for simply trying such a grand endeavor that she knew was almost beyond my psychological capabilities.

For the next three months (with the exception of a three-week vacation in June) I flew at least twice a week, sometimes three, learning the basics of flying. It took a solid two months for the voice in my head to stop telling me to quit this craziness. That nasty voice, disguised to think it was protecting me, kept saying, *Kim, you are going to kill yourself and John.* The voice was relentless. *Just don't go. Cancel the whole idea. What are you thinking? You don't need to learn how to fly. You can do lots of other things. This isn't important.*

I would wake up in the middle of the night, get out of bed, go to the glass doors, look outside, check the weather, and find comfort when it was cloudy and rainy; that meant I couldn't fly the next day. But so often I would wake up in the morning to find the weather perfectly fine for flying. Somehow I always got in the car to make the forty-five-minute drive to Elizabethton, despite that nagging voice.

I'm not sure John understood the extent of my fear. We didn't talk about it except that one time when we first met. But I can't imagine how anyone sitting inches away from me day after day couldn't sense it, especially when my hands would shake, my voice would quaver, and the handwriting I used to enter the date, the aircraft number, the Hobbs time in and out (the time the aircraft is in use), the tach time in (the total number of revolutions performed by the engine), and the pilot's name, all of which needed to be written into the Skyhawk's required flight logbook, was almost unreadable. I would nod my head at every instruction without saying a word. I tried to comprehend, register, and execute everything John taught me. Sometimes I got it; lots of times I didn't. Sometimes I would do the exact opposite. Often times I heard my nice voice encouraging me. *You'll get it, Kim, or, You got this. No problem.*

During the forty-five-minute drives to the airport, I would call the Elizabethton AWOS (automated weather observation system) two or three times. That's what pilots do, check the weather. Each new week I learned the value and importance of another element of the AWOS. At first and for a while, I didn't understand how to apply the information the report was providing. More importantly, I didn't even know what some of the words meant. But in time I realized the report's value, how each element relates to another, the inferences that can be made to determine additional valuable weather information, and increased my vocabulary.

Procedures eventually become routine and automatic. I started saying with an unconvincing confidence, "Don't worry, John, I'll get us there," particularly when the approach to land was all wrong. I would be too high or too low, give too much power, not enough power, have airspeed too slow or too fast on final. My execution of the controls was seldom coordinated—a critical skill for a pilot. Every adjustment created some sort of result that I didn't have the experience to anticipate. But I always got us on the ground safely, even if we bounced two or three times down the runway.

Other times I'd come in for a landing with the airplane sideways. One wheel would touch down. Then the other wheel, forced by gravity, physics—whatever natural phenomenon exists—would touch down screeching and pivoting us safely along the runway. Finally the nose wheel would bang onto the pavement. A silent wave of relief would ripple through me as I swallowed the lump of tension that had been building up. Unintentionally but aggressively, I would hit the brakes to slow the roll out. Both John and I would take the bouts of whiplash in stride. Not often, but every once in a while, I would perform that sideways landing with the grace and finesse only a lucky beginner could pull off.

I even managed to get us in situations that required a missed approach because I missed the runway. No, no, no, I didn't land on houses, or on the street, or crash the airplane. I learned how to go around and try it again. In the end a missed approach became no big deal, it was just part of knowing how to fly in lots of unplanned situations, behaving calmly while executing procedures properly. But believe me, at first I was crumbling inside: my heart racing, blood circulating throughout my entire body at an exponential rate, genuinely terrified. Surprisingly, my brain did function intelligently with a focused command. How did that happen?

There were, however, several weeks during which I became proficient at doing everything wrong. It was reassuring and felt good in an odd and deranged way that I could still be alive (and keep John alive too) while performing so deficiently.

John, easygoing and a natural encourager, always calm, never uptight or emotional, said, "Kim, becoming a pilot is very special. You'll gain a lot of confidence. Very few people become pilots."

I thought, *Hmm, usually I'm a pretty confident girl. What if this crazy flying experience only makes me a less confident girl, when I fail to earn a private pilot's license?*

Solo

Before I was allowed to solo, I had to complete a pre-solo written exam and pass a medical exam. The pre-solo exam was thirty-eight questions, a take-home test. It wasn't easy, and it was time consuming. It took me an entire Sunday (which, by the way, was a gorgeous day) to complete! I found most of the answers in either my two-inch-thick Jeppesen *Guided Flight Discovery Private Pilot* textbook, or the twenty-five-pound 2013 *FAR/AIM* (Federal Aviation Regulations/Aeronautical Information Manual) book. During the next scheduled flight-training day, John and I looked over my completed exam and made corrections. It was all good, for the most part. I was inching closer to "solo day." What a scary thought that was.

For the next month we practiced the basics, particularly pattern work, over and over again. A pattern is a rectangular route that lays out certain procedures at the specific four points and intersections (crosswind, downwind, base, and final) when approaching an airport to land. Initially, learning the pattern was done on the ground. John drew out a few key mountains and a small lake and the two runways, six and two four, at Elizabethton. (Two four means the runway lies on the earth at 240 degrees (drop the last zero) almost due west, but more accurately west southwest. Three six is due north, or 360 degrees. Get it?

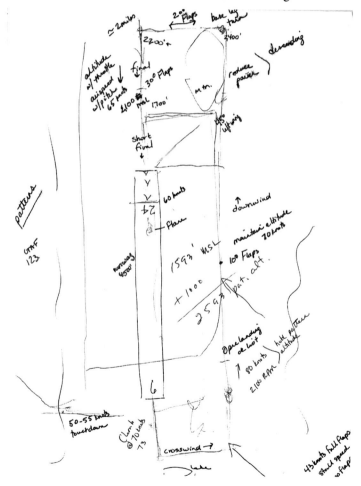

Each end of every runway has numbers in increments of ten identifying the direction in which the runway is heading. A pilot knows she is landing or taking off on the correct runway if the heading or compass matches the runway numbers.)

He also listed the airport altitude of 1,593 feet and added 1,000 feet to signify the flight altitude while in the pattern. As he spoke, I made notes on the diagram to help remember what to do and when. I memorized the pattern and all its particulars; I even ran it millions of times in my head during sleepless nights.

In addition to the pattern diagram, I began saying over and over in my head, because initially I just couldn't grasp the concept: *airspeed with pitch, altitude with power.* (I still say this over and over in my head and sometimes recite it out loud randomly while flying.) A pilot can efficiently control the airspeed with the up or down pitch of the airplane. Adding or reducing power also efficiently controls the altitude. I even thought about pasting a sticky note bearing my new mantra on the instrument panel, but I decided that would be too embarrassing!

We practiced patterns methodically, sometimes to the point of it becoming painfully boring. But I would eventually appreciate the wisdom of repetition.

It wasn't always pattern work. We ventured to several local airports, landed, and did touch-and-goes (landing on the runway and taking off again without coming to a full stop). During dinner I often explained my day's lesson to Gunther and Olivia.

"Guess what I did today, Gunther? Hit-and-runs," I bragged.

"You did what?"

"Hit-and-runs," I repeated.

"You mean touch-and-goes?" He corrected me.

His comment stopped me in my tracks. But not right away. "Uh no, hit-and-runs," I said again.

He tipped his head, then eyeballed me.

"Oh, oh, yeah. No, no. Yes, you're right. Touch-and-goes," I said, moving beyond the incident like it wasn't as stupid as I realized. Blondes can do that.

We practiced short and soft field takeoffs and landings, go-arounds, slow flight, slips-to-land (a skill used to dissipate extra altitude without increasing airspeed above that required to land), hit-and-runs (oops, I mean touch-and-goes!), emergency landings, flying in controlled airspace (I still needed lots of work there) and even flying with a simulated engine failure. That was wicked awesome. I asked John if we could do that a couple more times. We did. How does that work? Okay, okay, I'll tell you, because I know every one of you armchair pilots is dying to know.

Each time, but particularly the first time John went through the simulated engine failure drill with me, my senses were sharp and keen to every single word he said and each move of the controls he made.

"During any flight always look for an emergency landing area, an airport, an open field, or a highway, for example. Always be prepared. Do as much planning as possible," John explained.

So, we're cruising along at 4,500 feet MSL (above mean sea level) when John said, "Kim, I'm going to reduce the engine throttle to idle. The propeller will continue to rotate. Understand though, that during a real engine failure the propeller may continue to rotate as a result of the airplane's forward movement and the air flowing over the blades. The Skyhawk's best glide rate is 65 knots. We need to establish and maintain that airspeed with pitch and flaps. Look for a suitable landing area. Attempt to restart the engine. If that doesn't work, change the carburetor heat knob. Set the fuel selector valve to Both. Make sure the primer stick is set and locked. Enrich the fuel/air mixture. Set the ignition switch to Both or Start. Communicate 'mayday' on frequency 121.5. Squawk 7700 (which means the airplane is in distress). Just prior to landing, be sure your seat belt is secure, and the fuel selector, the mixture, and the ignition are all off (to help prevent a fire). Unlatch the doors for easy and quick escape."—Yikes!—"Adjust the flaps as required, and turn off the master switch. But above all, FLY THE AIRPLANE. Nothing is as important as flying the airplane."

While John slowly and thoroughly explained the engine out checklist, I performed every task, short of communicating "mayday," squawking 7700, or having to escape. I felt the airplane slow and become sluggish. Confidence and determination consumed me, and adjusting the pitch and flaps was constantly needed, but made all the difference in the world, like life or death. We glided for miles above the beautiful Appalachian Mountains, over her ridges and into the long corridor valleys of Tennessee in complete control. I spotted the Elizabethton airport and entered the left base of the approach pattern for runway six. I added power and we cruised through final, landing safely.

Simulating an engine failure reduced my fear tenfold. It was a turning point, a game changer, an epiphany. If something as catastrophic or potentially fatal as an engine failure were to ever happen while I was at the controls of an airplane, I knew now that I had the knowledge and, more importantly, the experience to work my way toward safety.

There were many times we went to Shady Valley, the designated practice area, or other practice areas to do fun stuff, like dizzying 45-degree bank turns, clearing turns, turns around a point, climbs, descents, climbing turns, descending turns, pilotage (navigating by comparing ground reference points to aeronautical charts), and low flying. One day we flew 500 feet AGL (above ground level), following a winding backcountry road in Virginia. I felt like a Bond girl.

But John made me do the not-so-fun stuff too, like power-on and power-off stalls. Stalling an airplane is when the angle of attack increases to the point at which air can't smoothly pass over and under the wing, and the disrupted airflow no longer generates enough lift to support the airplane. During stall practice, a loud piercing horn went off, and the airplane began to fall. At that point I immediately pushed the nose down and then added power. Those procedures increased the airflow around the wings, created lift, and forced the airplane back to flying. I'm good with stalls now. Sort of.

The second requirement prior to soloing was obtaining a flight physical from a certified FAA medical doctor. Officially it's called a Department of Transportation Federal Aviation Administration third-class medical certificate and student pilot certificate. I scheduled my appointment with Dr. Davant, a second-generation family doctor practicing in Blowing Rock, North Carolina. I'd never seen him before. Gunther sees him, and saw his father before him for his flight physical.

Blowing Rock is a modern-day mix of Norman Rockwell's Stockbridge, Massachusetts, and Andy Griffith's Mayberry, North Carolina: a combination of sophistication and a homey, grassroots, mountain mentality. The Blowing Rock hospital is not modern. It's nostalgic of an earlier time. I arrived at the Blowing Rock hospital a little nervous, not about passing the physical, but because I would be another step closer to having to solo.

I hung out in the waiting area alone. Soon enough a nice lady, local for sure, called my name and then escorted me to an exam room.

"Someone will be with you shortly," she said.

The door was cracked, and a different nice lady peeked her head in, then left.

Another nice lady came in, took my vitals, weighed me, read the chart, and said, "Oh, you're the FAA," and left.

Another nice lady came in, read my chart, and said, "Oh, you're the FAA." She left.

Each nurse always left the door slightly ajar.

I was a little confused. And then, between all the ins and outs of my exam room, the fire alarm went off. No one got excited or told me to gather my belongings and leave. Everyone remained in the building, with no urgency to exit or find shelter from a potentially life-threatening occurrence. So I just sat in my exam room, shrugged my shoulders, and continued to read.

Another nurse came in and again said, "So, YOU'RE the FAA!"

Still unaffected, I followed her to another room, where I had my vision and hearing examined, among other things. All was good. She took me back to my initial exam room. I waited a very short time and in came Dr. Davant, a short, roundish, fair-skinned, rosy-cheeked man, accompanied by a young female intern. The fire alarm quit. He introduced himself along with the intern and explained her presence.

He said to the intern, "This is Kim, and I'll be doing an FAA flight physical. This is a little unusual; we don't see many females getting a flight physical."

Then I got it. When those nurses had entered my exam room, they hadn't been expecting a woman.

During the exam, Dr. Davant explained that the physical is fairly superficial. The FAA wants to make sure that a pilot doesn't have any illness or condition that could suddenly impair his/her ability to fly. After my physical, Dr. Davant described me as "disgustingly healthy." He filled out the required FAA paper-work, and in no time I was holding my ticket to soloing.

I was excited, but apprehensive . . . and on the schedule to fly with John the very next day at nine a.m. If all went well, I could be soloing tomorrow.

The previous few weeks, the guys at the airport had been saying to me, "It won't be long till you solo, Kim."

Every time I heard that, I said, "One step at a time. We'll see," while I was thinking, *OMG—they're stressing me out. I can't solo!* But I did feel a sense of comfort from their easygoing confidence in me. Plus I liked them, and I knew they were sincere.

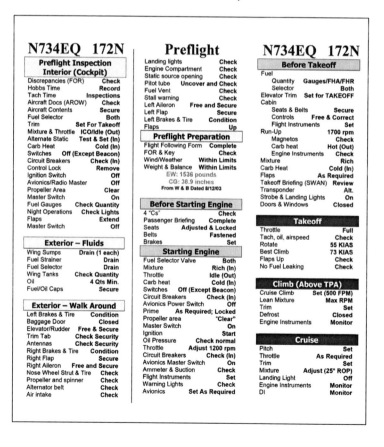

N734EQ   172N

Preflight Inspection Interior (Cockpit)	
Discrepancies (FOR)	Check
Hobbs Time	Record
Tach Time	Inspections
Aircraft Docs (AROW)	Check
Aircraft Contents	Secure
Fuel Selector	Both
Trim	Set For Takeoff
Mixture & Throttle	ICO/Idle (Out)
Alternate Static	Test & Set (In)
Carb Heat	Cold (In)
Switches	Off (Except Beacon)
Circuit Breakers	Check (In)
Control Lock	Remove
Ignition Switch	Off
Avionics/Radio Master	Off
Propeller Area	Clear
Master Switch	On
Fuel Gauges	Check Quantity
Night Operations	Check Lights
Flaps	Extend
Master Switch	Off

Exterior – Fluids	
Wing Sumps	Drain (1 each)
Fuel Strainer	Drain
Fuel Selector	Drain
Wing Tanks	Check Quantity
Oil	4 Qts Min.
Fuel/Oil Caps	Secure

Exterior – Walk Around	
Left Brakes & Tire	Condition
Baggage Door	Closed
Elevator/Rudder	Free & Secure
Trim Tab	Check Security
Antennas	Check Security
Right Brakes & Tire	Condition
Right Flap	Secure
Right Aileron	Free and Secure
Nose Wheel Strut & Tire	Check
Propeller and spinner	Check
Alternator belt	Check
Air intake	Check

Preflight

Landing lights	Check
Engine Compartment	Check
Static source opening	Check
Pitot tube	Uncover and Check
Fuel Vent	Check
Stall warning	Check
Left Aileron	Free and Secure
Left Flap	Secure
Left Brakes & Tire	Condition
Flaps	Up

Preflight Preparation	
Flight Following Form	Complete
FOR & Key	Check
Wind/Weather	Within Limits
Weight & Balance	Within Limits
EW: 1536 pounds	
CG: 38.9 inches	
From W & B Dated 8/12/03	

Before Starting Engine	
4 "Cs"	Check
Passenger Briefing	Complete
Seats	Adjusted & Locked
Belts	Fastened
Brakes	Set

Starting Engine	
Fuel Selector Valve	Both
Mixture	Rich (In)
Throttle	Idle (Out)
Carb heat	Cold (In)
Switches	Off (Except Beacon)
Circuit Breakers	Check (In)
Avionics Power Switch	Off
Prime	As Required; Locked
Propeller area	"Clear"
Master Switch	On
Ignition	Start
Oil Pressure	Check normal
Throttle	Adjust 1200 rpm
Circuit Breakers	Check (In)
Avionics Master Switch	On
Ammeter & Suction	Check
Flight Instruments	Set
Warning Lights	Check
Avionics	Set As Required

N734EQ   172N

Before Takeoff	
Fuel	
Quantity	Gauges/FHA/FHR
Selector	Both
Elevator Trim	Set for TAKEOFF
Cabin	
Seats & Belts	Secure
Controls	Free & Correct
Flight Instruments	Set
Run-Up	1700 rpm
Magnetos	Check
Carb heat	Hot (Out)
Engine Instruments	Check
Mixture	Rich
Carb Heat	Cold (In)
Flaps	As Required
Takeoff Briefing (SWAN)	Review
Transponder	Alt.
Strobe & Landing Lights	On
Doors & Windows	Closed

Takeoff	
Throttle	Full
Tach, oil, airspeed	Check
Rotate	55 KIAS
Best Climb	73 KIAS
Flaps Up	Check
No Fuel Leaking	Check

Climb (Above TPA)	
Cruise Climb	Set (500 FPM)
Lean Mixture	Max RPM
Trim	Set
Defrost	Closed
Engine Instruments	Monitor

Cruise	
Pitch	Set
Throttle	As Required
Trim	Set
Mixture	Adjust (25° ROP)
Landing Light	Off
Engine Instruments	Monitor
DI	Monitor

Unable to sleep, I ran the Elizabethton airport pattern in my head over and over and over again, forward and backward: runway six then runway two four. From four a.m. to six a.m. I considered winds, sun, birds, etc., etc., etc. I thought of everything important and everything unimportant. *There's no reason John wouldn't let me solo today,* I thought. In my mind I was ready. I knew I could do it. Thankfully I caught an hour's sleep between six and seven. I arrived at the airport just before nine a.m., pre-flighted (checklist on previous page), and off we went.

A flight instructor never tells you in advance when you're going to solo. Supposedly when they are comfortable with your abilities and your mental and psychological competence, they'll ask you to pull over, tell you you're ready to solo, and step out of the airplane. That day was like every other, not much chatter between John and me—we just got down to the business of flying. It was a cloudy day, and the winds dictated runway six. I preferred runway two four, but I'd have to make six work if I did get to solo that day. There's a weird bit of unstable air above the tiny lake when flying over short final to runway six, which made me slightly insecure.

When we were on pattern number six—no, number seven—actually, I think we were on our eighth pattern (it seems I lost count), I was thinking, *Is this guy going to let me solo or what?* I was getting tired and the clouds were sinking. *Okay, we're now on pattern number ten, for sure!* I was starting to perfect my mistakes, and my landings were getting worse with every additional pattern we flew. *He'd better get out soon!* I even looked at John a few times, my eyes piercing the words, *You can get out now. I can do this.* I was going crazy inside.

Finally, after what must have been twelve takeoffs and landings on runway six (John will surely disagree with the number of patterns we did that day. But that doesn't matter! This is my story.), the clouds were sinking. We were holding short for our thirteenth pattern and I was about to transmit over the radio "Elizabethton traffic, Skyhawk 734 Echo Quebec"—that's the identifier, or tail number, of my airplane; *echo* is for *E* and *Quebec* represents *Q*—"departing runway six *again*, Elizabethton," John said he was getting out.

Thank goodness! It's about time, I thought.

He said with calm assurance that instilled confidence and security in me, "Kim, you're ready to solo. Do three patterns, then come back to the terminal."

WHAT? Three patterns? That wasn't part of my plan. *No one ever told me I would have to solo THREE times ALL BY MYSELF. I was prepared to solo ONCE!* a voice in my head snapped.

I quickly got over the change of plans and focused on the task at hand. I was anxious but not scared. I hadn't realized how comforting John's presence was until he got out and I was ALL ALONE. The feeling of emptiness in the airplane was eerie and lonely; John's six foot two and 225 pounds, so he took up quite a bit of space in my tiny Skyhawk. (Okay, it was not MY Skyhawk. It belonged to the airport. But when I flew it, it was my Skyhawk.) But no worries, I just pretended he was there the whole time.

Every minute, I talked out loud to myself: "Flaps up, carb heat in, mixture rich, ready for takeoff. Full power, rotate at 55 knots, rudder. Holy cow, this thing took off quick; it just popped into the sky and off the runway. What's up with that? Something's wrong!" Later, I found out that 225 pounds less weight in an airplane that small makes a real difference in its handling. Despite the quick takeoff, everything appeared to be okay. Back to flying: Climb at 73 knots. Communicate. "Elizabethton traffic, Skyhawk 734 Echo Quebec's turning right crosswind, Elizabethton."

Look outside, check for traffic. Climb to pattern altitude 2,800 feet and maintain 80 knots. Communicate, "Elizabethton traffic, Skyhawk 734 Echo Quebec's turning right downwind, runway six Elizabethton."

"Moving along—patience. Keep an eye outside, scan instruments. Reduce power to 2,100 rpms, 70 knots, 10 degrees of flaps. Pre-landing checklist: fuel's good, trim set, cabin is secure, mixture's rich, carb heat is out, flaps as required." I was still talking out loud. I envisioned John right next to me. *Altitude with throttle, airspeed with pitch. Descending to 2,400 feet. Communicate.* "Elizabethton traffic, Skyhawk 734 Echo Quebec's turning right base runway six, Elizabethton."

Twenty degrees of flaps, descending to 2,200 feet, reduce power. Communicate. "Elizabethton traffic, Skyhawk 734 Echo Quebec's on final, Elizabethton." *Thirty degrees of flaps, 1,700 rpms, slow this thing down. Approach at 65-70 knots, over the threshold, flare just beyond the numbers, land at 60-65 knots. Keep the airplane straight, a little rudder, ailerons, touchdown, nice and easy. Greaser! Yes, I did it, great landing. Gentle run out.* I let out a huge sigh of relief. I'd landed. I started to breathe again. *Communicate.* "Elizabethton traffic, Skyhawk 734 Echo Quebec's clear of runway six, Elizabethton."

Two more patterns to go.

I got through the next pattern seamlessly. On the second landing, I bounced once, but got the airplane down. There was a lot of tension, anxiety, and stress, but I had done it so many times that truly it was automatic.

I was lined up on runway six and ready for the third and final pattern in order to complete my solo requirement. I transmitted over the radio, "Elizabethton traffic, Skyhawk 734 Echo Quebec's departing runway six, Elizabethton."

I took inventory, assessed the instruments, and took a look outside, ready for takeoff.

"Wait a minute! I can't see the mountaintops. John said THREE patterns! But I can't see the mountaintops. Kim, you're the pilot in command. John said THREE patterns! But I can't see the mountaintops." I was arguing out loud with myself. "I can't fly. I'm required to stay clear of clouds. If I take off I'm going to get in those clouds. I'll panic and crash Dan's airplane. He'll be very upset with me, but I'll be dead."

What do I do? I'll call Unicom.

Timidly, I got on the radio. "John, this is Kim, I can't see the mountaintops. What do I do?" I waited for a response. And waited. And waited. NO RESPONSE. He was not answering me. *No one's answering me! What do I do?* I was nervous. Really nervous. John said THREE patterns. I pushed the throttle forward with my right hand, worked the rudder pedals to ensure a straight takeoff, and held the yoke with my left hand in anticipation of liftoff. My eyes moved from the airspeed indicator to outside the airplane and back again. All the while EQ was speeding down the runway, gaining momentum.

A voice said firmly in my brain, *Kim. You can't. See. The mountaintops.* I pulled the power back, and the airplane decelerated.

I was relieved. But I hadn't accomplished the requirements. *Oh well, I'm alive! That's the requirement as far as I'm concerned!*

John came over the radio. "Kim, what's the matter?"

I said nervously but with confidence, "John, I can't see the mountaintops."

"Okay, let's call it a day. You did great," he said

I enjoyed a second round of relief and taxied back to the terminal.

I soloed! It counts.

The first thing I did when I got inside the terminal was text Gunther: *Did it!*

He immediately called me. He was super excited and so proud.

I texted Krista: *Soloed!*

She replied: *?*

Oh for goodness' sake, she doesn't know what soloed means. So I texted her back: *I flew the airplane by myself.*

She replied: *OMG, Awesome!! Were u scared?*

Was nervous.

I was so excited about soloing that I told everyone, particularly my flying friends (who are really Gunther's friends, but since I'd been flying, they were now my friends too). They didn't just hear that I soloed, they had to hear my entire story, every dramatic detail. Everyone was so excited. I felt like they were proud and even impressed. It was fantastic.

What I didn't expect, but realized after the third or fourth person I told, was that everyone had a story of their first solo, and they wanted to share it, too. I would finish telling my story, almost out of breath with excitement, when most would reply with, "Wow, that's great, Kim. When I soloed . . ." I heard everything from "When I soloed fifty years ago at the age of seventeen just before going to war . . ." to "When I soloed it was easy. I just wanted to get it done so I could move on, get my license." Each reply would steal my thunder. I thought, *Hmm, that's great for you, but what about me? I'm the one who just soloed and my story is better! It's more dramatic, more exciting, more dangerous, more everything!* But naturally, I reacted with excitement and great interest in their experiences. I like to listen. Plus, I learned a lot.

Flying seems to bring together unlikely people, allowing us to connect and bond over our shared passion. It's like a special club, and the only requirement for membership is flying. Imagine two people, complete opposites, who don't even like each other.

But somehow the fact that they are both pilots comes out, and instantly they bond and begin to converse like they're old friends. Weird.

Who would have thought I would even have made it this far and into that club? Not me. I can assure you of that.

I soloed and I still couldn't believe it.

CHAPTER TWO
Therapy

John has a tendency to randomly take trips at the last minute; sometimes these coincided with my scheduled flying lessons. One day, he said, "Kim, while I'm gone, it's a good time to fly outside the pattern. Fly around a little bit." He made it sound like flying an airplane beyond what I deemed within my safe limits, by myself was a normal progression and an easy task. Well, it wasn't!

I knew the Elizabethton airport pattern intimately. I knew exactly where the airplane needed to be, and when. I told John that flying even one inch outside the pattern was frightening to me. I'm not sure what he thought about that, but my guess is that, this far into his teaching me, my expressed emotions probably went in one ear and out the other!

Ten hours of flying solo is one of the many requirements to earning a private pilot's license. With John away, I decided after exhaustive internal debate to take the airplane up by myself and fly a few patterns. It was not a perfect day for me to be flying. But weather conditions were above minimums for VFR (visual flight rules). VFR required me to have visual reference to the ground and other aircraft. At this point, a novice pilot like me has to conform to VFR rules. Flying in weather requires the knowledge and use of flight instruments or IFR (instrument flight rules). I don't know how to use those instruments yet. I assessed the weather and decided I could get in some pattern work. The clouds were high enough over the mountaintops for me to have good visual, and the winds were under ten knots. I pre-flighted. My hands were shaking and my adrenaline was pumping. I was scared, like always. Regardless, I took off on runway six; the crosswind leg of the pattern was clear of clouds. Ahead on the downwind leg, a cloud moved directly in my path. Then lots of clouds surrounded me, creating a situation that could potentially leave me with no choice but to enter clouds. That's a no-no. A student pilot must always stay clear of clouds because we have to be able see to avoid other aircraft and/or terrain. The ceiling, or the lowest layer of clouds above the ground or water, was low, but above the mountaintops. *What do I do?* I thought. My life momentarily flashed in front of me. *Should I call the Unicom, talk to Dan? What's he going to do? He'll only prolong my decision-making. He's not up here at 2,800 feet. He can't logically help me. I have to figure this out.*

I've NEVER veered off the pattern course by myself, not even an inch! I can't fly a wider pattern because the clouds are closing in on me. I can't ascend. Clouds are up there, too. The only option is to fly a narrow pattern, to my right, close to the runway. Is that allowed? I quickly answered myself out loud. "When it's the only option, it's allowed!" Fearing for my life, I turned to the right, rounding the clouds. I was directly over the runway and flying the wrong way over the final and base legs of the pattern. Up ahead, where I needed to turn for the base leg just prior to final, the clouds were hovering high enough for me to feel the slightest bit of hope. If I could just get out to the base leg where the clouds were well above my pattern altitude, I could turn around, and I'd be okay. *Clouds, please don't close in on me anymore.* I saw the opportunity to zigzag back to the corner of the base leg. I turned base and headed for final, landed runway six, taxied to the terminal, shut the airplane down, and got out. Psychologically I was broken, but more thankful than any other time in my life to be alive.

I walked through the terminal, dropped off the flight log book without a word to Fulton, an Elizabethton Municipal Airport employee who was working the administrative counter, and kept going straight to my car. I drove to McDonald's for a Coke, and texted my experience to John. His response was, *Good decision making, that's what a good PIC* (pilot in command) *does.* That's all he texted back. No excitement, no drama to add to my drama, no questions, nothing!

When I got home, Gunther got a play-by-play of the entire experience with all my emotions. He always listens and reacts with encouraging support. However, he offered no sympathy for my being scared, and with all confidence in me, reiterated that I have the mental strength and discipline needed to be a pilot. Weakness is useless, but a tiny bit of fear is healthy, he comfortingly reasoned.

I questioned my sanity after those kinds of experiences but never let them deter me. John was gone another time, maybe to the beach. Nevertheless I was up in the air again, working on patterns and landings. I was just flying by myself, not veering from the routine of pattern work. I transmitted over the Elizabethton airport communication frequency, which is monitored by all air traffic in the area, "Elizabethton traffic downwind for runway two-four."

A Citation jet transmitted over the Elizabethton communication frequency, "Eight miles out, inbound for runway six."

Did he not just hear me?

Runway six and runway two-four are on the same landing strip. We are on a collision course. The Elizabethton airport is an uncontrolled airfield where no traffic controller exists, therefore pilots communicate with each other under the visual flight rules. Every pilot understands and complies with VFR rules. It keeps us safe.

I transmitted over the Elizabethton airport communication frequency, "Left base runway two four."

Citation transmitted over the same frequency, "Five miles inbound runway six."

I was a nervous wreck. This guy was playing chicken with me. With lightning speed, I reviewed my Jeppesen private pilot textbook in my head, pulling up every VFR I had ever learned. I recalled the airplane in the pattern has the right of way. The airplane at the lowest altitude has the right of way. That was me! According to VFR rules, I was first in line to land. I had the right of way.

Apparently Citation didn't care about VFR, never mind flying etiquette or just plain old manners. *What do I do, what do I do?* Clearly he was experienced, since he was flying a Citation jet and wasn't worried about a runway collision, which was sure to occur if I landed. I was just a student—a nervous, petrified student. My mind raced with potential options: I could extend my downwind, so he could land. But I'd never ever been even an inch out of the pattern alone, except for when I was forced to avoid clouds in order to save my life. Remember?

I pressed the mic button on the yoke and with calm control in my voice (but physically and psychologically near a melt-down), I said, "Elizabethton traffic, Skyhawk 734 Echo Quebec extending downwind for inbound traffic, Elizabethton."

Can you believe Citation had the nerve to respond? He said, "Thank you, appreciate that. Citation on final runway six." He hadn't specifically talked to me once throughout this entire high stakes experience . . . until now. The nerve! This pompous Citation just bullied me, little Skyhawk, right out of the pattern. I bet to this day that Citation pilot doesn't even know what he put me through. He probably has no idea that he was violating VFR, uncontrolled airspace rules.

Out of nowhere, a surge of confidence came over me. Instead of turning base and landing after the Citation, that voice I like to gravitate toward said, *Kim, go to Shady Valley.* I had been there hundreds of times (okay, maybe not quite) with John. It's the practice area. Without flinching, I added power, retracted the flaps slowly, and reversed carb heat. It must have been divine intervention again.

I headed to Shady Valley a confident yet nervous wreck. I reviewed the instruments, scanned the horizon, listened to the engine, and then calmly looked outside. I saw the beautiful land below, the tire of the airplane, and I felt comfortable—but only for a split moment. I continued over Cross Mountain and arrived above Shady Valley. Slowly and ever so softly (because I was afraid to do anything abruptly), I put pressure on the left rudder, rotated the yoke, and gently began the turn back to Elizabethton. This sounds basic, but it was a big deal to a new pilot. Willingly and alone, I went beyond the pattern. *Yay me!* I felt good.

If I hadn't been bullied by that Citation, it surely would have taken me longer to voluntarily venture beyond that inch! Regardless of the Citation's inadvertent positive influence, I knew he'd been in the wrong. With disgust in my voice and my tone begging for support, I told my Citation story to those who would listen. To my surprise, everyone was reluctant to reassure me. I guess they had to assess the situation, think about it, and ponder what I had done wrong. Whatever! Always an excuse and due respect for the experienced guy. I got over it. (Not really! I just have to say that so I don't sound spiteful.)

Cross-Country Solo

When I first began learning about the requirements of obtaining a private pilot's license, I thought a cross-country was literally flying across the country—like to California from North Carolina.

That would cost a lot of money in fuel and airplane rental costs, I thought. Surely someone will have to go with me. And then back again! That'd take a lot of time. More time than I've got. I have a family. I gotta go to work. Gunther will never go for that.

Immediately when I worried aloud about a cross-country trip, I was laughed at and teased. "No silly, a cross-country means a round-trip flight of about 150 nautical miles with several stops in between." Even though it was way shorter than I had initially imagined, it seemed like an unfathomable exercise for someone like me.

Flying a cross-country solo was the next requirement to earning a private pilot's license. Keep in mind that I had just recently soloed for the first time, and was by no means psychologically ready to fly by myself on a regular basis, never mind undertaking a long solo cross-country flight!

Thankfully acquiring the skills to fly an airplane can be learned one baby step at a time. I was attempting my very first short cross-country solo flight to the Virginia Highlands Airport. It was about twenty-five nautical miles away, and I figured that it would take me eleven minutes, plus an additional ten minutes to climb and descend each way; therefore, a round-trip of about forty-five minutes. No big deal. I'd traveled to Virginia Highlands lots of times with John.

But that discouraging voice crept into my head again. It said convincingly, just like it did back in May, *Kim, quit this craziness. With no instructor, you are going to kill yourself! Just don't go. Cancel the whole idea. What are you thinking? You soloed. That's enough. Be proud; move on.*

But my encouraging, confident voice calmly answered back, *Kim, go on. You have the fundamentals. You understand the procedures; there's no reason to feel insecure.*

I'd rescheduled this trip three times because of uncooperative weather. I'd practiced the procedures and memorized all the ground landmarks for three days straight. My brain was exhausted. It felt like I'd never so intensely and continuously studied in this serious and diligent way before.

The day arrived and the weather was just right. I went through the routine: a preflight walk around, preflight check-list, run-up, takeoff, headed for Shady Valley, turned left over the mountain ridge, cruised over South Holston Lake, looked for the Virginia Highlands Airport, and called Virginia Highlands traffic about five miles out. I was by no means calm. Apparently over the radio, I appeared calm and confident—so I'm told. Once I flew the approach pattern and was set to land runway two four, I took a look outside. There was the runway, directly below me. *Crap, I can't land. I'm way too high and halfway down the runway. Oh my gosh, missed approach!* I quickly, nervously recalled the missed approach procedures. Since I'd managed to get John and me into lots of missed approach situations, practice should make perfect—right?

I executed the missed approach procedures as I'd routinely done in the past, but without any instructor to guide me or provide security. I went around for a second time. *Fly the approach; crosswind, downwind, base, final.* I took a look outside. *Altitude is good. Oh no! You have got to be kidding me? I am right of the runway and a quarter of it is behind me. Here we go again. Another missed approach.* I went around for a third time. I was disgusted and embarrassed that I had to communicate yet another missed approach. *No time for emotions. Get it right, Kim.* I went around again. This time I landed safely. I cleared the runway, taxied to a temporary parking location, and began the process of calming myself down.

It took a while.

My right leg was shaking uncontrollably, and my hands were

white. My muscles, my veins, my ligaments, my arteries—every part of me that could collapse was lethargic and jellylike. My spirit was in shock. My entire existence was exhausted and relieved. I had just unintentionally executed two missed approaches! Not one but two, by myself, alone, solo.

Never in all my life were the stakes that high or the emotions so physical. Only when I won a gold medal and became the best in the world for a day (in the giant slalom at the Junior World Alpine Championships at Alyeska), was the reward that profoundly consequential. And that confidence John had been talking about? Well, I felt it.

I had to slowly and methodically pull it together. More challenges lay ahead. In preparation for the return flight, I dialed 0A9 (Elizabethton Airport identifier) into the GPS. It said my route was 5,000 miles away and at a heading of 280 degrees. I said to the GPS with disgust, sarcasm, and calm, "I really don't plan to fly to Russia. Plus I don't have enough fuel to go that far, and it's cold in Russia." I was thinking about what it would be like to be stranded in Siberia.

What's wrong with me? I've done this so many times. This has NEVER happened. Okay, let's reenter the information. Same thing. I tried again and again. Same thing: 5,000 miles away and a heading of 280 degrees. *How ridiculous.*

Thank God for my gentle, reasonable voice. *Kim, you know the way home. You don't need the GPS. Go on.*

Okay, that's right. I do know the way home! I can get back to Elizabethton without the GPS. Off I went.

I settled into cruising altitude, grateful to be on my way back to my home airport. I tried entering 0A9 into the GPS again. *It's giving the same heading that I'm flying and the distance makes sense. It's working! It's working!* Yes, I did something right! It's working! I was excited and, for a tiny moment, proud. And then out of nowhere I realized my mistake. This time I had correctly dialed in a zero like the number zero instead of an *O* like the alphabet: *L, M, N, O.* Big difference!

My first attempt to land in Elizabethton was a success. Like always, unless I had a crazy experience, after I secured the airplane, I walked to the ground instruction room in the Elizabethton Municipal Airport, logged my time, and found solace in texting Gunther, Krista, or John—oftentimes all three. A Coke from the McDonald's drive-through was the second phase of post flight therapy.

During the forty-five-minute drive home, the third phase of therapy began. Every detail, every emotion, every experience, every physical motion that was crystal clear in my head, I put on paper. That writing was the origin of this book. With a pen in my right hand, paper laid out on a magazine across my lap, whenever it was safe I would jot down the day's experiences. In between driving and writing I stole a sip of Coke or scarfed a bite of my cheeseburger.

I never ever considered turning back on becoming a pilot. I was determined to push forward. The fright and the fear were rooted deep within me, but the challenge was sensibly addicting.

Two days later, on September 6, I flew the same short cross-country solo route again. It was a gorgeous, clear fall day, sixty degrees, with winds at 110@4 (the wind was coming from the southeast at four nautical miles per hour). And to add to the beauty of the fall day, I landed on my first attempt in Virginia Highlands! But not before communicating that I was nine miles to the northwest, when I think I was really nine miles to the southwest. *You are such a ding-dong, Kim.* Oh well. I was a bit calmer, a little more composed, and had a stronger feeling of inner security on that flight.

However, there was never a dull moment, at least not on this flight. When a pilot enters the airspace of an uncontrolled airport, he/she will first obtain the automated weather observation system (AWOS) on an assigned radio frequency to determine the wind direction, altimeter setting, the visibility and sky condition, the temperature, the dew point, and any other remarks. This information aids in determining the landing strategy.

Next, the pilot will dial in the Unicom/traffic communication frequency in order to listen to and speak with other aircraft in the airspace. I attempted from memory to change the Elizabethton AWOS and Unicom/traffic frequencies to the Virginia Highlands airport AWOS and Unicom/traffic frequencies. But my memory failed me. I fumbled nervously with my paperwork, read my notes, and tried to identify the correct frequencies. At last, I dialed in the correct radio frequency numbers. Virginia Highlands (KVJI) weather was coming over the radio loud and clear. Then, I switched over to the KVJI Unicom. I heard other traffic in the area and gave a sigh of relief.

Wind direction dictated runway six—I'd never landed in that direction before. I flew perpendicular over the runway (John recommended that), entered a left downwind, adjusted power, altitude, and speed, and went through the pre-landing checklist. I turned base and was fighting with the convergence of each approach element: flaps, rudder, altitude, carb heat, power, wind, communication, everything! They didn't want to come together and coordinate. I was on final and too high. *Plenty of runway, Kim,* John's voice said in my head. That statement would always subtly remind me that everything was okay. Things aren't always perfect but they can work. I landed—good enough.

During my climb out from KVJI back to 0A9, I reviewed the initial leg of the trip in my head to adjust and execute corrections. The trip back was uneventful. The nice linemen at 0A9 were always welcoming after my exhausting trips, even if the trips themselves were only 40 nautical miles round-trip. One of the guys was always there to direct me in, chock the Skyhawk to prevent accidental movement, and ask if I needed anything. Sometimes this gave me the chance to talk about the trip. Routinely, I headed to the ground instruction room, filled out my logbook, destressed, and texted somebody. The process settled me before I got into my car, then stopped at the McDonald's drive-through.

Long Cross-Country Solo

Never in a million years did I think I would solo, never mind solo cross-country. In the days leading up to my planned long solo cross-country trip, I drummed up all kinds of coping tactics.

"Hey John, do you think that I could stuff you into my back pocket during the required long cross-country solo? I won't tell anyone. No one will know, not even the FAA. What do you think? Sounds good to me," I asked, wishing it could happen.

John didn't react. I bet inside, though, he was smiling, maybe even chuckling a little bit.

My cross-country plan was to travel from Elizabethton, Tennessee, through the Tri-Cities (Kingsport, Johnson City, and Bristol), Tennessee, controlled airspace (where I have to talk to and execute the traffic controllers' instructions), to Gatlinburg, Tennessee, to Morristown, Tennessee, back through the Tri-Cities controlled airspace, and then back to Elizabethton. I was nervous on that early morning drive to 0A9 from home. I kept trying to distract my mind with music, at the same time reviewing procedures and the route. I called the automated weather observation service at each airport at least three or four times.

It was a beautiful, brisk fall Saturday morning: 45 degrees, sunny, with calm winds. All summer long, temperatures had been in the 80s and it was often humid. It had been so hot that sweat regularly dripped off me in the airplane, because the Skyhawk lacked air conditioning. Yuck. But that day the temperature was inviting and I dressed warmly in jeans. I brought a hat with me, just in case. And during every milestone in my piloting adventures, I had inadvertently worn a purple short-sleeved shirt. I realized this just before my long cross-country. But it was cold out, so not a day for a short sleeve. No matter. The first layer was my purple short-sleeved shirt, then a thin, long-sleeved turtleneck, then a zip-up sweatshirt. (I'm not superstitious—ha!)

I arrived at the Elizabethton airport just before eight a.m. and pre-flighted. All was good. I was still nervous, but suppressing it well. I had time to spare, so I sat on the couch, watched TV, and waited for John. I think we'd made plans to meet at eight thirty, with plenty of time for me to depart at nine. John arrived, reviewed my navigation logs, and signed my logbook. I think he sensed that I was nervous, but nevertheless, he proceeded as usual—matter-of-fact, but conveying comfort and a calming assurance. All he said to me was, "Do good."

Okay, I can do that, I thought. To the airplane I walked. *You can do it, Kim. No problem. Focus on the procedures*, I kept telling myself.

John was on the ramp, texting, talking, fiddling with his phone. He does that a lot. I detoured over to him before boarding the airplane.

"John, I'm going to take runway two four, okay?" I asked, trying to find one last bit of reassurance. The winds were variable. That meant I could take off on whichever runway I preferred.

He broke away from his iPhone briefly to say, "Okay, Kim." *Whew! He's good with that.* He showed no signs that what I was about to do was HUGE.

I boarded the airplane, went through the checklists, apprehensive, but deep down—way, way, way deep down—the confidence was there. I took off at 9:10 a.m. for my first-ever long cross-country solo trip.

Once I was clear of the Elizabethton traffic area, I called Tri-Cities approach since I was flying through their airspace. And at my request the Tri-Cities traffic controllers would be providing me with flight following. That means they would be watching out for me, letting me know if other aircraft were in the area, alerting other aircraft of my position and providing any other flight advisories. At any time during my flight I could cancel flight following. But why would I? They're sort of like human angels, offering assistance and guidance.

The traffic controller replied, "4 Echo Quebec, squawk 4072."

A squawk is an assigned code given to the pilot by the first encountered traffic controller. The pilot enters the code into their transponder. This assigned code or "squawk" gives all traffic controllers the ability to identify and monitor an airplane at all times: where they are, what altitude they're flying, the direction they're flying, etc. A pilot can change the transponder code to communicate various messages by using specific codes; for example, there's a code for an emergency, a code for when radios fail, a code for a hijacking.

"Tri-Cities approach, squawk 4072, 4 Echo Quebec," I repeated.

"4 Echo Quebec, I'm not receiving you," he said in a hurry.

"Okay, Tri-Cities approach, I'll cycle the transponder," I responded.

They were not receiving my transponder transmission. A pause in communication ensued for some time. I wasn't worried. I was flying VFR at 4,500 feet, it was beautiful out, with no wind, no turbulence—no big deal.

It had been four months since my introductory flight; I had flown lots of times with and without John.

Tri-Cities approach called me: "Echo Quebec ident."

IDENT? What the heck does that mean? Thinking, thinking, thinking, still thinking. Nothing, I got nothing. Well, I better respond somehow. "Tri-Cities approach; I'm a student pilot on my first long solo cross-country. I don't know what ident means," I said.

"4 Echo Quebec, there's a small red button on your transponder. Push it in," the controller replied.

Okay, nice guy! Feeling some relief here.

"Tri-Cities approach, 4 Echo Quebec, I did that," I said.

"Echo Quebec, I'm still not receiving you," he says, like it's my problem, which it is, but not really a problem. I was flying VFR (according to VFR rules I'm responsible for *visually* locating traffic and steering clear), so it wasn't necessary to have a transponder. Just an extra safety, a backup. That's what flying's about, lots of backup when preparation isn't enough.

I responded, "4 Echo Quebec."

Other than the "ident" issue, the flight so far was going as planned.

Prior to initiating this milestone, John required that I prepare navigation logs using sectional charts and those stone-age tools I bought on day one to aid in my calculations, which Gunther had no choice but to go through thoroughly. I know I tested his patience a lot. He earnestly checked every calculation a couple of times. Today sophisticated GPS instruments and even my iPad calculate routes by simply entering the proper data.

"Are you sure that's right? Check it again," I questioned as though my life depended on it.

I didn't feel the navigation logs and the sectional charts were enough. I needed more. I wrote out a three-page narrative of the flight from start to finish—another solo cross-country coping tactic. It included what to say when to traffic controllers, landmarks I should see below, points at which I should execute certain procedures, frequencies at each airport, altitudes I should cruise at, headings, distances—a surplus of detail. It was imperative that Gunther and John read it over. This was my personal security, my backup. I can't help but wonder if both of them thought, *Who does this? This girl is nuts.*

The three-page narrative was proving to be a useful tool, though. It relieved each concern and worry that I could potentially drum up. Landmarks, mileage, headings were all checking out. I even experimented a little with the VOR, a VHF Omni-directional Radio Range. For a novice like me, it's a confusing navigational instrument that receives a signal indicating my position in relation to a specific VOR (a transmitter, a ground station, or a beacon) like Holston Mountain or Snowbird.

Gatlinburg was coming up, my first planned landing. *Where's the airport? What runway do I take?* Adrenaline was slowly creeping into my system. I spotted the airport. My position and orientation to the airport was confusing me, though. The wind was telling me I should land on runway two eight. Traffic was using runway one zero. *What?* I was talking to myself. *Why are they doing that?* My adrenaline rose several notches higher. *Okay, I'll follow traffic.* But I couldn't get all my flying components to converge. Airspeed, altitude, pitch, timing, and my communication were all over the place. My mind was racing. But the calm, reasonable, life-saving spirit inside me discreetly entered the back door. *Turning base. Speed is low, add power. Runway coming up quick. Way high. Plenty of runway, Kim* (that's John's voice). *Descending, descending, speed's too fast. I'm descending, halfway down the runway already. Too high, not enough runway. And in a hundredth of a second I'm going around. Pitch up, add power.*

"Gatlinburg traffic, 4 Echo Quebec, I'm gonna have to try this again," I communicated. My adrenaline was maxed out, but my survival skills kicked in. *I gotta execute procedures. Slowly milk the flaps up, ten degrees. They have to come up slowly, or else I can lose lift and drop out of the sky.* Gulp.

I was in the pattern for the second attempt. I went through the pre-landing checklist, talking out loud. "Carb heat, crap, forgot to add carb heat. Thank goodness for pre-landing checklist." Without the carburetor heat the engine could freeze up, making me a goner.

My adrenaline was off the charts now, but I was still in control. My heart was pounding outside of my chest. I set up better for landing that time, but it was still awful. *Who cares! I'm on the ground!*

I taxied off runway one zero and proceeded to runway two eight. I still had the wind issue, though. Traffic was landing on runway one zero. But the windsock was telling me to take off from runway two eight. I didn't want a tailwind for takeoff. I departed runway two eight for Morristown, Tennessee. All was good. I switched weather and communication frequencies for Morristown. Wind said runway five. Traffic agreed. *Great!* Relief at last.

There was lots of traffic at the little uncontrolled Morristown airport. I kept listening. The traffic chatter didn't quit. Airplane after airplane kept calling downwind, base, final. All I knew to do was to properly communicate, and let them know of my position and intentions. So that's what I did. Seamlessly I flew 4 Echo Quebec into the pattern and in among the heavy traffic. I was feeling some pressure to get on the ground the first time. Determined, I got it right and landed on the first attempt—but not without a high bounce and a long float.

I started to sweat on this beautiful, cool, fall day. The temperatures warmed, and it was by this point about 10:15 a.m. When I cleared the runway, I looked around. *What in the world is going on? Airplanes everywhere: old ones, single-engine airplanes, a jet, biplane, war airplanes, people, kids, concessions! You have got to be kidding! An airshow is underway!? Like I don't have enough to manage! That explains the heavy traffic and constant chatter inbound. Get me out of here.*

I taxied back to runway five. I was number two for takeoff, after some sort of old-timey, open-cockpit biplane. A nice single-engine was behind me, and more airplanes behind the single-engine. Is this for real? I was in Morristown, not at JFK. Everyone had told me: flying's about adjusting. Not only was I in line for takeoff, but I had to wait for incoming traffic. *Good grief.* This may take a while.

More often than not, Gunther prepared my sandwich the morning of a flying day. This time, though, I had prepared and packed my lunch. Since I had time waiting for my turn to take off, I ate my homemade chocolate-chip-oatmeal-raisin cookie, a bunch of bush beans, and drank some water. I reviewed my narrative, sectional chart, and navigation logs for the next and final leg. I was feeling a tiny bit of pride and satisfaction. I was three-quarters of the way there. I had almost conquered this huge, huge, very huge requirement. Mentally I paused, when that reasonable voice said, *Not so fast, Kim, you still have a quarter of the trip ahead of you. Extinguish those thoughts and remain focused. Do not step out of the present and into the future of predetermined accomplishment.* Yup. I understood.

I was ready to taxi onto the runway for takeoff. *But wait, how much space am I supposed to give the biplane that just took off? When can I take off?* Neither my friendly, informative Jeppesen textbook nor the obnoxiously large and confusing FAR/AIM book ever told me explicitly how much space to give an old-timey biplane before I could safely be permitted to take off. I've learned about the wake turbulence of jets. This was still uncontrolled airspace, even with an airshow going on. There were no departure controllers, and no instructor to guide me. *It's just us airplanes. The guy in front of me isn't going to tell me when I can go. The guy behind me isn't going to nudge me forward. Wake turbulence shouldn't be a factor. Biplane's too little.* I just eyeballed it, meticulously.

Once the biplane took off, I waited, waited, waited. I noticed he was heading in the opposite direction of where I intended to fly. I strained my eyes to see if I could see him anymore. Okay, he seemed clear. I should be good to go. I followed him out. But I was super cautious, mindful of trying to execute every procedure properly. The airplanes behind me were probably thinking, *Go already! What are you waiting for? It doesn't get any greener.*

Full power, manage pedals, rotate at 55 knots—I'm off. Climbing nicely. Heading home. Finally the airways were silent, peaceful. For the first time during the entire flight and for only a few moments, I sat back in my seat. I held the yoke with ease instead of the stranglehold that would suffocate a baby chick, scanned the instruments, and took a look outside. It all looked and felt familiar. Those inviting mountains, the safety of those valleys, that rich green late-summer foliage, and the long strips of flat farmlands along the North Carolina / Tennessee corridor below comforted me.

With contained excitement, I got a little choked up—okay, I got completely choked up while rapidly blinking my eyes in order to clear the tears dripping down my face. I whispered with relief, "There's Chimney Rock." Chimney Rock is a VFR checkpoint, a definitive mountain landmark close to home that John had pointed out during the two practice runs we did together. It's clearly marked as a checkpoint on my sectional chart. It was all coming together!

I contacted Tri-Cities (KTRI) approach, since I would be entering their TRSA (terminal radar service area) airspace. I knew the drill, but I was still tentative, and not 100 percent comfortable with all of the communication terminology and procedures within controlled airspace. The approach controller recognized me from my earlier communication from 0A9 to Gatlinburg. That was reassuring, plus the guy was nice to me. He let me know that there was traffic at two o'clock and 4,000 feet. I didn't see it, but I let him know I was looking. I told you those controllers are human angels.

Oh, there it is! I see it.

"Tri-Cities approach, 4 Echo Quebec, I have the traffic in sight," I replied.

"4 Echo Quebec, does he look like he's at 4,000 feet?" the controller asked.

What? He's asking me a question, like I'm for real, a real pilot? He wants ME to let him know what I think! Does he know who he's talking to? That I'm a student pilot on my first long solo cross-country, exceptionally insecure, yearning to safely reach my destination and have this experience well behind me?

By now the aircraft was at about three o'clock just above, in the distance beyond my wingtip. I checked my altimeter and compared his position to my instrument reading.

"Tri-Cities approach, 4 Echo Quebec, from what I can tell he looks like he's at 4,000 feet."

I had just told an air traffic controller what I thought! I was a real pilot! In a trance, I slowly shook my head, and tried to dissipate the lump of disbelief in my chest.

Here we go again: just like before on my way outbound from 0A9 to Gatlinburg, the Tri-Cities controller lets me know that my transponder's not communicating a signal. *No stress, just go with it again.*

"4 Echo Quebec your transponder's not communicating a signal. Ident," the nice guy from Tri-Cities approach reminds me.

"Tri-Cities approach, 4 Echo Quebec ident," I said.

"4 Echo Quebec, I'm still not receiving you," he says.

"Okay, 4 Echo Quebec."

I kept flying along, scanning the instruments and the horizon while vigilantly listening to the radio traffic. I saw the landmarks and the familiar terrain that surrounds the Elizabethton airport just ahead.

"Tri-Cities approach, I have the Elizabethton airport in sight," I communicated to the nice traffic controller.

"4 Echo Quebec radar service terminated. Good day," the nice traffic controller replied.

No way, I made it through the controlled airspace intelligently. Is that not official? Again I said to myself, "I am piloting an airplane."

"4 Echo Quebec, thank you. Good day," I replied with humble confidence and an unbelievable feeling in my heart and soul.

Winds are calm at 0A9. I'm going straight in runway six. Home FREE. I landed, bounced, added power, floated, landed, and cleared runway six.

I was all choked up. I could barely communicate. "Elizabethton traffic, 4 Echo Quebec clear of runway six," I transmitted, with a quaver in my voice.

I sat for a moment. *I did it: my first long cross-country solo . . . And I NEVER EVER want to do it again.* My nerves were shot. I was mentally lifeless and physically exhausted from the self-induced tension.

I pulled out my phone while taxiing to the terminal. *I've got to tell Gunther.* I texted him, *On the ground at 0A9, holy cow. I did it.*

A helicopter was active, ready to depart on the west side of runway six. This was an unusual position for a helicopter at Elizabethton.

Dan came over the radio, "4 Echo Quebec, 0A9 hold short for that helicopter." In other words: Don't move, wait for the helicopter to depart. *You should know that, Kim.*

Oh geez. I fumbled with my cell phone and replied, "Elizabethton traffic, 4 Echo Quebec, of course, holding short. I apologize."

The helicopter took off, and everything was good. Don't text and taxi!

Alex, the young, blond, and often serious lineman, who does just about any task required at a small airport—like open the airport headquarters in the wee hours of the morning; move, manage, and fuel airplanes; make coffee; chase animals from the runways; talk with big-wig luxury airplane pilots who happen to fly in or out; reserve rental cars for incoming guests; and help student pilots—was on the ramp. He directed me in and safely parked me. I shut down 4 Echo Quebec. Alex gave me a thumbs-up, chocked the airplane, asked if I needed anything, and then moved on to his next task.

I gathered everything from my Skyhawk and headed inside. It was a Saturday, so there were lots of guys hanging around at the airport, and the staff was behind the counter. John and Daniel were there waiting to take 4 Echo Quebec (EQ) up. Daniel was one of John's other students who was about a month ahead of me in training. Showing signs of mental and physical exhaustion, I plopped my bag down next to them and give a brief summation of my trip. I received lots of sincere congratulations.

Done. That's it. The long solo cross-country is under my belt. I still don't ever want to do it again.

I headed to the ground instruction room, recorded the trip

in my log book, and called Gunther. He was wicked excited and super proud. He told me that he and Olivia had listened to me on www.liveatc.net and that I sounded professional and calm. I was glad to hear the joy in his voice.

The day was not yet over. I still had an hour and a half in the backseat of EQ. John and Daniel, who was doing the first portion of his practical test training, invited me to go along. Daniel's a North Carolina State Trooper, plus he got a ninety-something on his written exam. It's always an advantage to be friends with the smart guy. The flight was exactly what I needed to calm the excitement from my first long cross-country solo.

It had been a long day, and after four hours of flying, I headed home. I cried for most of the way, tears rolling down my cheeks. I made no effort to hold them back. I wiped them off, stopped crying for a moment, thought about the day, and then started crying some more. This went on for thirty minutes. They weren't tears of joy, but rather tears of relief and accomplishment. Krista and I texted back and forth during my drive home when the opportunity arose. She was really supportive and so complimentary, like a twin sister should be.

After four months of stress, tension, and fear, I finally allowed myself to appreciate the fact that I could really fly an airplane. When I got home, the exaggerated emotions began again, and I cried some more. Olivia and Gunther were compassionate and consoling, but I'm sure they thought I was a nut case! Who cries about accomplishment?

CHAPTER THREE
Listen, Observe, and Learn

Daniel and John invited me to fly with them again the day after my long cross-country, from five to seven p.m., while Daniel completed the second and final phase of practical test training. I sat in the back of the airplane, completely relaxed and glad someone else had the responsibility. Plus, the security of an onboard instructor was doubly comforting. All I had to do was listen, observe, and learn.

In the air John ran Daniel through a battery of test maneuvers: under the hood (instrument training), unusual attitude, slow flight, power-on and -off stalls, circling a fixed ground point (which happened to be the FAA examiner's house—funny, huh?), short field landing, and power-on stall in a steep bank to potential spin. Did you just get that? POWER-ON STALL IN A STEEP BANK TO POTENTIAL SPIN! Explicitly, that means that the aircraft rolled at a very slow speed toward a vertical, nose down, slanted position. Once the airplane began to slip John maneuvered it into forward and level flight. Good thing because we could have spiraled faster and faster in a corkscrew motion to the ground! THAT was intense and a little unnerving to say the least. I had never experienced or practiced this maneuver. I was physically and mentally holding the airplane in the air from the backseat; my hands were white knuckled, gripping whatever was within reach; my feet were planted on the floor—all while praying more sincerely than I had ever done before. I'm not sure if I became lightheaded from the physical maneuver, or if it was a result of sheer fright. The other two pilots I'm sure had no idea what I was up to in the backseat.

John was completely in control for the maneuver. We came out of it like any other simple exercise. Well, *they* did. I closed my eyes, sighed, and gulped as secretly as possible, melted into the back of my seat, and thanked God the three of us were okay. The guys were fine, and nonchalantly they moved on to the next piece of business.

All in all, it was a fantastic way to learn. Daniel nailed everything John threw at him and appeared to be at ease, at least from my vantage point. His confidence and solid execution taught me that I needed to be more assertive. I realized that I was much too timid as a pilot.

The two of them took a short break after landing. For the next two hours, from seven to nine p.m., it was my turn to work on instrument and night flying. I pre-flighted and found 4 Echo Quebec was low on oil. *How come I always have to refill the oil? 'Cause the other pilots just don't do it.* I added oil. Everyone was in the airplane. Daniel came along to get in his final two required night landings after I completed my night training. Off we went. I was the pilot in command, John was right seat, and Daniel was in the back.

Gosh, it took forever to get airborne, because even though I'm little, the two guys are big. I guess their weight shifted about. And the airplane kept swaying, so I had to work the rudder pedals hard to keep the airplane speeding straight down the runway. Once we reached maneuvering altitude, probably 6,500 feet, I put on the foggles and began instrument work. Foggles are glasses that restrict your vision, so all I could see was the instrument panel—nothing outside. John flew the airplane into certain situations. At a given point or time, he would calmly

(John's always calm, never gets uptight or expresses extreme emotion) instruct me to make specific adjustments, using only the instruments. We did this "under the hood" work for about an hour. It wasn't hard at all. I liked it. John said I did "good."

By now the sun was down, the sky was clear, and the wind was nonexistent: ideal conditions for night training. I did eight of the ten required night takeoffs and landings, and even had a greaser, which is when the landing is smooth and gentle, like landing perfectly on soft butter. One fun exercise was remotely turning on the runway lights with the mic button, which is located on the yoke of EQ. One minute the ground below was pitch black, and then out of nowhere a little airplane with a girl in awe of her experiences clicks the mic five times and lights up the runway. How magical is that?

It was getting late. I landed. Daniel and I traded places. He took control of the airplane and completed his final two night landings with ease. At about 9:15, the three of us completed the long but productive day. I recorded the session in my logbook and headed home.

A Bundle of Nerves

For practice I was to fly from the Elizabethton Airport to the Tri-Cities Airport, the TRSA (controlled airspace), and back solo.

En route to the Tri-Cities Airport, the approach controller cleared me to land runway two three. I visually identified what I thought was runway two three. Without cross checking my compass I was headed for runway two seven. To my surprise it turned out, though, that two seven was closed. As soon as I spotted the extra-large X on the runway, I figured I was headed for the wrong landing strip. I quickly made the forty-degree change and landed on runway two three. Whew! That would have been embarrassing. But my landing wasn't good either. I bounced, floated, added power, and eventually touched down permanently. Once I landed, I had to ask ground control to repeat the taxi instructions. I can only imagine what those controllers were thinking or if their heads were rolling on the floor from shaking them so hard in annoyance at my inexperience!

While taxiing I saw Gunther, a bunch of guys, and our airplane on the ramp at Wysong, a helicopter refurbishing company that specializes in avionics and electronics. *Oh good grief,* I thought. *I hope they didn't see me head for the wrong runway and then land twice on that one attempt. I can't pay attention to them; I need to focus.* I did. With a disastrous experience like that, flying into controlled airspace from here on out would be intimidating.

The controllers were very patient and nice, but I was a wreck. In heart attack mode waaay too often, I wondered if I was developing heart problems. I did have the wherewithal to jot down the departure instructions, though. I took off and headed home, with radar contact until I had the Elizabethton airport in sight. Landing at the Elizabethton Airport was still bad. I came in too fast and as a result bounced once or twice.

Gunther texted me and said I did well, and everybody including him was impressed. REALLY? That made me feel better about the experience. His next text said I sounded calm while communicating, and that my recovery on the landing was well done and my communication was very good. Recovery! That's how I landed all the time these days. Nonetheless, his text made me smile a tiny bit. But somehow his assessment didn't match my reality. Apparently he knew I was flying in and he and his buddies rigged up a handheld radio out on the ramp, so they could listen to me while watching me blunder through the experience. Cute, wasn't it?

On the way home, I read over my texts and replayed the

day's flying in my head. Alone in the car I laughed and laughed at the fact that a pilot in the sky (me) was heading for a closed runway, botched every communication procedure, bounced down the runway, almost got lost while taxiing, and still had the nerve to continue flight training. At this point in reading my book, I'm sure anyone who has wondered about taking flying lessons is probably petrified to get in the air, knowing that there are crazies like me in the sky. But surely I can't be the only pilot who makes mistakes or feels insecure?

Written Exam

I had been studying for the written exam for a couple of weeks. I read the entire written test guidebook and did 80 percent of the test questions contained therein. Daniel directed me to a few written exam practice test sites online. I'd been practicing those test questions over and over as well.

One evening I had a meltdown. I was exhausted from studying during my every free moment, day after day. I was getting questions wrong much too often and I was just plain tired of the repetition and dedication that was needed. I dropped my head to the table, pushed my books away, and devoted some time to feeling sorry for myself.

I know crap!

I can fly the airplane all by myself, not just around the peapod of Elizabethton, but to three different airports, through controlled airspace. I can handle missed approaches, recover from challenging landings, perform a long list of maneuvers, add oil to my airplane, comprehend an AWOS report, turn on runway lights for a night landing, land at night, and execute basic instrument flying, all with a level of proficiency and confidence I never thought I would attain. But I can't pass a written exam? It's over! I'm quitting. $6,000, five months, and fifty hours of training, all down the drain.

Every question Gunther helped me with I got wrong, in addition to the ones I did myself. Okay, that's an exaggeration. But he was *supposed* to know every answer right off the top of his head immediately. After all, he's been flying since the late '70s, owns his own airplane, has 8,000 hours logged, he's an FAA A&P and an IFR commercial pilot, so how could he get questions about a private pilot's license wrong!?

During this time, I was mean, impatient, and just plain rotten to Gunther. There seemed to be no solution other than to quit. I decided for one night to set the studying aside. The next day arrived. I was reenergized and receptive to learning while he was patient and willing to help. Thank goodness, because I really need his support. That afternoon and into the night I maturely reread sections of the written test guidebook, and practiced the online questions over and over until I mentally couldn't digest another word.

I called the test center at the Tri-Cities airport to schedule an appointment to take my private pilot's written exam. Inconveniently, but not to my surprise, the guy at the test center said that I had until Friday, October 4, to take my written exam, because after the fourth, all test centers across the country would be closed indefinitely due to the government shutdown. Well, *okay* then! I'd be taking my exam on October 4 at one p.m.

I had been studying for two weeks now and flying for five months, but I still felt pushed and under pressure.

Something Clicked

The day before my written exam, I had a psychological and mental breakthrough during my flight training session with John. For reasons unbeknownst to me, I flew with about half my usual stress level. It just happened. Something clicked.

I'd been working diligently and repetitively on proper

approach to landing, flare, and touchdown. Previously, I just couldn't consistently get in a smooth landing. Then John and I tried something new. Twice, just before landing on short final (about a mile from the runway), John took control of the airplane. I followed along on the pedals and yoke, diligently scanned the instruments, and then focused my eyes outside while John demonstrated two perfect greasers. An instructor's supposed to get it right, right? Most importantly at the final landing phase, just over the runway numbers and shortly prior to touchdown, I realized I needed to fly about 20 feet above the runway, flare ever so gently with reduced power, have the airspeed at 59/60 knots, hold the nose up firmly, and let the airplane glide softly to the ground.

I couldn't help but remember that introductory flight when I had my hands and feet barely on the flight controls, with no intention of applying any pressure or making any moves short of breathing for fear of inadvertently causing the airplane to suddenly plummet from the sky. Now, I was fully engaged in the process and found it wonderfully challenging, even addicting.

Test day! Had I really gotten to the point of taking the written exam for my private pilot's license? It was all so surreal, like I was a windup toy and I hadn't run out of batteries yet, and my direction was purely mechanical. I was just going and going, without comprehension of what I was in fact doing. I wondered, *How in the world did I get here from being so afraid five months ago?*

I'm in the test center sitting in front of the computer screen. *"Click to begin your test."* Question one appears. I don't know the answer. My heart is beating fast. *Okay, take a deep breath, slow down, read the question, read the answers. Kim, you know this stuff.* My supportive, reasonable voice prevailed! *There are sixty questions, and two and a half hours to do this. Plenty of time.* Sooner rather than later, I settled in. The questions became familiar and the answers made sense. At least some of them did. I finished in an hour and a half.

In order to get my score, I had to click the Finish button. I couldn't do it. Anxiety and near hyperventilation had set in.

Seventy or better is passing. With fear, I clicked Finish. My breathing stopped. I closed my eyes and prayed to God that a seventy or better appeared. I opened my eyes and looked at the screen—*You have got to be kidding me!* A questionnaire stared me in the face! I answered the questionnaire with disgust and disdain, but also fairly and honestly. (Typically I skew questionnaires by answering them with sarcasm and cynicism just to prove that a face, a human body, real feedback is so much more valuable than a worthless piece of paper containing obscure and false data.)

Here we go again—click Finish. Same drill: pray to God, eyes closed. Open my eyes: 77. *No way!* Life stopped.

I passed! The relief was so overwhelming that I almost collapsed. I was so happy . . . and scared to be proud for just a moment.

I left the room to get the test proctor so we could finish things up and I could leave. He wasn't immediately available, so I fetched my phone and purse. (They take that stuff away from you during testing.) I called Gunther, texted Krista, my older sister Sherri, my brother Erich, Erich's wife Zoe, and John. Soon enough the test proctor finalized the test, gave me my score sheet, and I was outta there—on cloud nine and overly excited.

As soon as I was in the solitude of my car, I called Mom and Dad; Mom wasn't home. But Dad just listened as I rambled on and on. Finally when I gave him a minute to speak he said, "Wow! That's great, Kimmie!" in his heavy Austrian accent. That's all I let him say, before I started rambling again. Finally, I let him get off the phone, but not before saying, "Be sure to tell

Mom, OKAY? Don't forget, tell Mom as soon as she gets home."

Gunther, Olivia, and I went away for the weekend to relax. They needed it as much as I did.

Oral Exam

I was hoping to have my private pilot's license before winter set in. I flew nearly twenty hours over the next three and half weeks with and without John, practicing the final requirements in preparation for my oral and practical exam with the FAA examiner. Many of the maneuvers weren't new, but certainly performing them convincingly in order to demonstrate that I had command of the airplane was a goal I needed to attain. Exercises like short and soft field landings, steep turns, all kinds of stalls, emergency landings, basic instrument flying, cross-country navigation, pilotage, dead reckoning, and night flying were some of the maneuvers I worked hard to perfect. Greasing a short field landing was rewarding, and realizing I could land an airplane safely without an engine was super-duper amazing.

John arranged an introductory flight with Wayne Timberlake, the FAA examiner who would be administering my oral exam and check ride (practical exam). John thought it would be a good idea to meet him and get a feel for his expectations. But it was another experience to worry myself about.

I flew 4 Echo Quebec from 0A9 over to KVJI where Mr. Timberlake is based, parked the airplane, and walked into the terminal, looking shyly for a stranger I'd never met before. John assured me that he was a fair examiner, but gave me no other info. *What does a fair examiner even look like?* I had spoken to Mr. Timberlake on the phone previously and had the impression in my head that he'd be a little, skinny, dark-haired, older gentleman.

I inquired with the guys at the front desk. They said they hadn't seen him. I sipped water from the water fountain and then took a seat in the lounge. I nervously tapped my foot on the floor and watched a few private airplanes take off and land. I got up again, walked back to the front counter, and there I ran into Mr. Timberlake: a medium-height, light-skinned, older, round, and very pleasant sort of a gentleman. We introduced ourselves. He said to call him Wayne. I noticed he was fidgety and shuffled as he walked.

He took me into his small, windowless office down the hallway. We got acquainted and he asked, "What do you need to work on?"

I honestly answered, "Well, I'm not real confident with steep turns or short field landings."

"Okay," he said. Then he went over exactly what he expected. "When I teach a student, I expect perfection. When I perform a check ride, I expect the minimum requirements," he told me in a very nice way.

He sounded like my kind of guy. I could do both of those for sure! I did a quick preflight inspection, and then we got into the airplane. Wayne made himself comfortable and even overtook some of my space before settling in. Once we were secure, I began to taxi—a little too fast. "I don't want you to exceed ten knots while taxiing," Wayne said. He gave me a few more pointers, like ensuring my nose wheel rode directly over the centerline while taxiing, and he adamantly informed me that I should always perform a magneto check prior to every takeoff. (The magneto creates the electric power for the spark plugs— no magnetos means no power. No power means no engine. No engine means no flying.) You'd think he'd be making me nervous with all this constructive criticism, but he wasn't. I was taking it all in like a sponge, and thinking, *What else you got for me? 'Cause whatever it is, I can do it.*

We took off. Wayne explained thoroughly why two four is

the preferred runway at KVJI. In case of a missed approach or an emergency landing, the departure end of runway two four has fewer obstacles to contend with. I-81 and a few little hills are located at the departure end of runway six. He asked me to do a steep turn to the right and then to the left. I did them with no problem. I flew a few more requested maneuvers while he talked the whole time. I interrupted when necessary. Finally we headed back to KVJI, and I entered the pattern for runway six, apparently quite wide. About a quarter into downwind, Wayne interrupted himself with a hint of fun in his voice and said, "Kim, you don't need to fly into the next postal code in order to get there."

I chuckled and said, "But this is how I fly."

In Elizabethton, there is a lot of terrain to avoid (mountains hug the airport in every direction), and therefore the pattern is unusually wide and long. Wayne did explain why I shouldn't fly patterns too wide under normal circumstances. Being closer to the airport gives the pilot a better chance of landing safely in the event of an engine failure. I appreciated his explanation. It made sense.

We did a total of three landings and takeoffs, one short field. Short field landings require the shortest distance possible to land and maximum braking without skidding or tumbling down the runway. I thrived on the challenge of a short field landing. When I got it right it felt awesome. All went well except, upon run-out while still on the runway, I raised the flaps and adjusted carb heat. "Wait until you have exited the runway before you clean up the airplane," Wayne stated. There wasn't really anything wrong with me raising the flaps and adjusting the carb heat while still on the runway. It's just not proper procedure. It can create a distraction to the pilot.

"Oh, okay," I said, and waited until I was clear of the runway before cleaning up the airplane. Next, I began to transmit over the radio that I was clear of the runway.

"Take a look at your tail." I turned my head like an owl. "You are still on the runway. Your tail is hanging over the runway/taxi line. Be sure you are completely off the runway before you communicate."

My tail was about six inches still on the runway. I inched forward and transmitted over the radio, "Virginia Highlands traffic, Skyhawk 734 Echo Quebec clear of runway six."

I flew back to Elizabethton confident in my performance, and pleased to know that I would have an easygoing but thorough FAA examiner for my oral and practical exams.

The oral exam and check ride (practical exam) were all I had left to complete. Daniel, who coincidentally periodically patrols the state highways in Banner Elk, and who had earned his private pilot's license not long before, stopped by my work office just before his shift one day to help me prepare for my final exams. He was dressed in full North Carolina State Trooper uniform—he even had his gun, handcuffs, and all that other stuff fastened securely around his waist. He spent about an hour with me going over *everything* Wayne had grilled him on during his oral exam, and each required maneuver he made him do on the check ride.

I took two pages of notes while Daniel racked his brain to ensure he communicated every detail Wayne expected us to know. Daniel told me about the navigation logs I needed to prepare, the detailed knowledge I would need regarding sectional charts: vector airways, gray airways, heavy white areas, magnetic variation, difference between blue and magenta airspace, military operations areas (MOAs), minimum flight elevations within quadrants. He went over the endless symbols: private airport versus non-private airport, VFR checkpoints, ceilings in all classes of airspace, ground tower heights, dotted lines, solid lines. He listed additional information I should be prepared to talk about, including airport beacon differences, best rates and angles of climb, maneuvering speed, density altitude, pressure altitude, hypoxia, hyperventilation, medical certificates required for each class of license, P-factor, requirements in order to be current, privileges of being a private pilot, which direction to land in the event of an emergency landing on a highway (with the traffic, not against it), minimum equipment for a VFR flight and on and on and on.

I studied those notes and my practical test guide thoroughly. Gunther quizzed me when he had the chance, and John texted me tons of questions. In the meantime, I completed the required four hours of practical test preparation with John, and made several solo flights after flying with Wayne. Since Wayne's the FAA examiner, he was the one who would pass or fail me.

Late fall and winter were approaching fast. Acceptable weather days for a check ride were getting fewer as storms and wind were more frequent. The two-hour oral exam is typically followed by the check ride on the same day. Four, potentially five hours of being under the FAA microscope sounded like a lot to me.

About ten days after my flight with Wayne, I called to schedule the oral exam and check ride. He was agreeable, but not sure which girl he was talking to. He had flown with several students, including a few women over the past weeks. To jog his memory I said, "I'm the girl who likes to fly through several postal codes on approach prior to landing."

He paused, then said, "Oh yeah, you're the girl who flew very well."

No way—really? My FAA examiner thinks I'm a good pilot? Wow! This was a great sign and a needed confidence booster.

We set the grueling day for Thursday, October 31.

Fate was on my side. I drove to the Elizabethton airport early that morning. The weather was marginal. Nonetheless, I was determined to begin the final phase to earning my private pilot's license. Once I got to Elizabethton, I rechecked the AWOS. Ceiling and visibility were acceptable, but the forecast for wind shear was not in my wheelhouse. No one flies in wind-shear conditions, not even forecasted wind-shear conditions. Dan was at the Elizabethton airport, so I consulted him.

After reviewing the weather conditions once again, weighing all of the advice I had accumulated and considering my options, I decided not to fly that day. There was no way I was going to take on the possibility of wind-shear conditions, an oral exam, and a check ride. The latter two were enough to contend with. Plus, the pilot is always in command, so the final decision was mine to make.

I called Wayne. He agreed, no flying. But we did arrange for the oral exam as soon as I could get to the Virginia Highlands airport by car, which was several hours later. We met in his small, windowless office. I had my purple, short-sleeved shirt on. Thank goodness, because it got hot and stuffy.

Gunther packed my lunch that day. I made sure it was a whole sandwich and two cookies so that when lunchtime came during what I expected to be a very long day, I could offer Wayne some food and not feel uncomfortable eating in front of him while he starved. He declined my half sandwich. I was glad, because I was ravenous. He did accept the cookie though, placing it safely on a stack of books on top of his desk. I ate my cookie and kept eyeballing his.

I made it through two and half hours of airplane talk. Everything Daniel had briefed me about, Wayne threw at me. He asked me specifics, expected me to discuss concepts, explain and thoroughly demonstrate my understanding of a sectional chart, describe in detail my planned cross-country navigation log. A few additional heavy concepts included Bernoulli's principle (John taught me about Bernoulli's principle on day two of flight training. He even drew it on paper for me), the ins and outs of

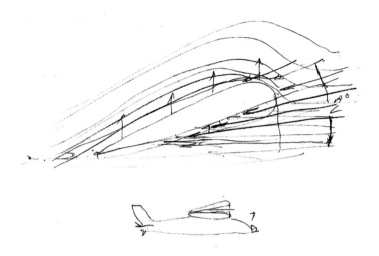

John's drawing of Bernoulli's principle: when the velocity of air increases, its pressure decreases. This is a key component of lift

carburetor heat (I pretended to know what I was talking about. Wayne caught on and explained it to me.), SIGMETS, AIRMETS (weather advisory information that contains meteorological information concerning the safety of all aircraft), and other facts like hijacking, radio failure, and emergency transponder frequencies. He asked me questions like what is an acrobatic pilot required to carry *(What kind of a question is that and who cares?* I had no idea and wanted to say, "Brains!" But I didn't. The answer is a parachute—that's comforting!), what color is your fuel, and what type of fuel and octane does your airplane use? (Blue, 100 low lead)

We began at about eleven a.m. Around 1:15 p.m., I asked, "Can we be done now?"

He said, "Yes."

"Okay, well, how did I do?" I asked.

"You did very well," he replied.

But I wasn't done yet. Like all pilots, without fail, they have to show you something: for example, an airplane! We loaded into Wayne's messy SUV and drove a very short distance to a hangar where he proudly showed me his teaching airplane. A green-on-white striped Cessna Skyhawk 172. It seemed like it had hardly been used and was fussily kept; not like *my* tired, faded, and overused but reliable EQ. His airplane stood tall and shined on the inside and out. I was impressed, and for a split moment I thought, *Wow, it would have been nice to spend the last five months in his 172.* But nothing could have taken the place of my EQ, especially since the eighty hours I'd spent in it had changed me profoundly.

The weather had deteriorated while I was cooped up in that little office. It had become cold, damp, and spooky—just what you'd expect on Halloween. Wayne and I looked at the weather forecast for the next few days, and tentatively penciled in a couple of dates for my check ride. As I departed, Wayne suggested I drive home north on I-81 through Damascus, the opposite way from which I'd come. I couldn't imagine what difference it would make, and I was exhausted, but figured I'd give it a try.

That evening, Olivia dressed up as Supergirl and we headed to Banner Elk's Halloween trunk-or-treat festivities. After passing my oral exam I felt like Supergirl without a costume.

The Check Ride

On Friday evening I called Wayne, who said the weather looked good for my check ride the next day. But several obstacles materialized. Gunther was scheduled to be in Virginia on business, which created a potential problem with Olivia. I needed to find someone for her to spend the day with, which I did. Plus, Wayne had scheduled a check ride with another girl. *Another girl! How awesome is that?* However, he assured me that both of us could indeed perform our check rides on the same day using the same airplane; we'd just have to jump through some hoops for it to happen.

The weather looked perfect in the morning but was forecast to deteriorate after one p.m. I drove to the Elizabethton Airport, flew 4 Echo Quebec to KVJI, and began my check ride at nine a.m. Katherine, a twenty-three-year-old, red-haired nurse from Johnson City, would drive her car to KVJI and perform her check ride in EQ at eleven a.m. *Isn't that great?* I thought. *A young girl has the confidence, the interest, the focus, the courage, and the discipline to become a pilot.* I was impressed. I'm still impressed. Once I completed my check ride, I would drive her car an hour from KVJI back to the 0A9. After she completed her check ride, she would fly EQ back to 0A9 and pick up her car. It was a confusing set-up.

My bag containing all the necessary items—headset, cross-country navigation log, sectional chart, E6B, flight computer, personal backup notes, phone, extra sweatshirt, lunch, and snacks—was all packed the night before. My night was restless. I woke up at six a.m. fidgety and nervous. Gunther was already gone. I ate a decent breakfast and prepared Olivia's, so that when she got up it would be waiting for her, and I would know that she ate a healthy breakfast. She was to spend the day with her cousins.

It was still dark as I left the driveway at 6:30 a.m. I looked at my watch. *Oh no, I have the wrong watch on. The one without the date! I need the date.* Pilots always record the date and hours flown in their logbook. Panic! *Kim, you don't have time to go back inside and get your other watch. Just go on. Everything will be okay.* I called AWOS continuously and tried to distract my mind with music, switching back and forth between my iPod and the radio. The sun was coming up as I entered Elizabethton at about 7:15 a.m.

It was a cold November day. Rough weather was brewing. I had dressed warmly, beginning with my lucky purple shirt. Jacob, the polite and friendly young lineman, was the only one at the Elizabethton Airport that early. Systematically but carefully, I pre-flighted in the hangar to stay warm. When I finished, Jacob moved the airplane outside onto the ramp.

4 Echo Quebec took me in like a familiar friend. I had been renting it almost twice a week for two hours each day since May, unless weather or maintenance grounded the two of us. Oh wait, the three of us. John was often part of our group too. Over the past six months I came to trust and respect both. The checklists were complete and by now the single engine was running. I placed my headset over my ears and flipped the master avionics switch on. There was no sound! I couldn't hear ATIS (automated terminal informational service: tells me which runway is active, some weather information, and other useful landing details and notices), AWOS, or me. I turned the avionics master switch off and then back on again, and troubleshot a while longer. With my

cell phone I tried to call Gunther. He was out of range. I texted John. He offered some ideas, but couldn't help either.

Never ever have I flown without communication, especially solo. VFR rules don't require communication, but it's a really good idea and a safety measure that I personally rely upon. Still I took off for KVJI at 8:15 a.m. without radio communication, because I was getting there that morning to perform my check ride, no matter what! That much I knew. All was silent, except the drama in my head: my nice voice and my doubting one. The flight was smooth. I landed fine, parked just outside the terminal, and walked inside to find Wayne.

I found him instantly and told him about my dilemma. As we headed to the airplane, he said he would have a look, mentioned a few solutions I didn't understand, but also implied that we might not be able to perform my check ride. Devastation filled me for a moment. Without missing a beat, I assured him that he could fix whatever was going on.

I did a stopover walk around before we both loaded into 4 Echo Quebec. After I turned the master power and the avionics switches on, Wayne fiddled with the audio panel and discovered that the radios were on Com 1, while the switch was either on Standby or Com 2. Problem solved. He explained the problem and the solution, and was surprised that I hadn't figured it out on my own. I wanted to hug him anyway.

I taxied well under ten knots, nose wheel dead on the center-line, and performed my magneto check. Humble fear was inside me, but lately the frequency and repetition of training always backed me up. I relied on that. During the preflight briefing, Wayne told me I was to fly my prepared cross-country route to the first checkpoint, which was five to seven minutes out. Takeoff was to be a short field. A short field takeoff requires the shortest runway distance using wing flaps and full throttle.

I reached cruising altitude of 5,500 feet and stabilized the airplane. I viewed the ground for landmarks. He questioned me on a few: a railroad and Interstate 81. I identified the first checkpoint: the intersection of I-81 and the two-lane road to Damascus. Then I realized why Wayne had suggested I drive home from KVJI via I-81 through Damascus when I'd seen him last. That was my first ground checkpoint—clever and indeed helpful! What a nice guy.

He instructed me to fly a 190-degree heading and descend to 4,500 feet. I did. Upon request, I performed a right-hand steep turn with no problems—but not before executing the required clearing turns first. Then I executed power-on and -off stalls. Stalls frighten me the most, but I kept it well hidden.

At 4,500 feet, Wayne noticed that there was a gap between the fuselage and my door. The door didn't appear to be shut all the way. He expressed grave concern. "We need to turn back, get on the ground immediately, and shut the door properly!"

"No, no, that's the way the door shuts all the time. It's secure. Don't worry. I won't fall out," I said. He took my word for it, but only after I twisted his arm. We continued the check ride.

I flew around a silo in the middle of a farm, but not very well. Then we moved over to his house, located on the banks of South Holston Lake, and he explained why a helicopter was sitting on the dock of his neighbor's house. (His neighbor uses it to go back and forth to work.) *Wow!* I thought while executing the required maneuver flawlessly. I was to circle his house from above. Between checking my instruments, viewing the horizon, keeping an eye on his house to ensure I circled it properly, trying to locate the helicopter on the dock, physically flying the airplane, and showing interest in his helicopter story, I had performed that ground-reference maneuver just fine.

Next I placed the foggles on my head. He gave me a heading,

said to descend to a certain altitude while maintaining a specific airspeed, and keep the airplane level. I aced that. I took the foggles off and Wayne said, "Most students have trouble with steep turns and instrument work. You did both very well."

Yes! I thought.

We were just about finished with the check ride when out of nowhere, Wayne suddenly took control of the airplane, jerking it to the right. Alarmed, he said, "Did you see that airplane?"

"No," I said calmly, but quickly scanned every window to see if I could tell what all the commotion was about. I felt like a well-trained fighter pilot. (*Top Gun*—you know!) "There it is!" I exclaimed. I saw it gracefully turning to the left in the opposite direction of our flight path, peacefully floating without a care in the world.

Whew, thank goodness. Alive one minute, dead the next. That's how fragile life is, I thought.

"It's a Saturday. Lots of weekenders are out for a joy ride," Wayne remarked with irritation. He told me to head back to KVJI and descend rather rapidly. I did.

When I have Gunther, John, or an FAA examiner with me, I can pretty much do whatever they tell me fairly well. It's the solo flying that challenges my confidence.

The weather was getting rough. The big change that time of year was wind. The little Skyhawk doesn't like strong winds, and neither do I. That's why when I smoothly touched down in ten knots crosswind gusting to fourteen on my check ride landing, I felt good. I must have passed.

I was sure to clear the runway *completely* before transmitting or cleaning up the airplane. Then I carefully taxied my precious cargo, Wayne, back to the ramp.

"Did I pass?" I asked timidly.

"You did very well. Let's head inside and finish up the paperwork," Wayne said.

Yes! I was happy, very happy. The entire world along with its weight was off my shoulders.

I was supposed to get a picture of myself and the airplane for Krista—for Facebook I'm sure. But I didn't have time for that. Neither did Wayne. He had another check ride with Katherine, so that request fell to the wayside. Wayne shuffled to the terminal. I secured the airplane, gathered my belongings, and followed him in. I wanted to skip.

Once inside the terminal, we ran into Katherine, and Wayne introduced us. How wonderful to meet a young pilot. I told her how amazing it was that she was becoming a pilot and wished her the best of luck on her check ride. She gave me her car keys and explained where her car was parked.

i. UNITED STATES OF AMERICA DEPARTMENT OF TRANSPORTATION — FEDERAL AVIATION ADMINISTRATION ii. **TEMPORARY AIRMAN CERTIFICATE**	iii. CERTIFICATE NO. PENDING

THIS CERTIFIES THAT   iv. KIMBERLEY LYNNE JOCHL

v.

DATE OF BIRTH	HEIGHT	WEIGHT	HAIR	EYES	SEX	NATIONALITY vi
5/18/1970	66 IN.	125	BLOND	BLUE	F	USA

ix.   has been found to be properly qualified and is hereby authorized in accordance with the conditions of issuance on the reverse of this certificate to exercise the privileges of

PRIVATE PILOT

RATINGS AND LIMITATIONS
xii. AIRPLANE SINGLE ENGINE LAND; [LIMITATIONS]: ENGLISH PROFICIENT

xiii.

THIS IS ☒AN ORIGINAL ISSUANCE ☐A REISSUANCE OF THIS GRADE OF CERTIFICATE	DATE OF SUPERSEDED AIRMAN CERTIFICATE 8/6/2013	
BY DIRECTION OF THE ADMINISTRATOR		EXAMINER'S DESIGNATION NO. OR INSPECTOR'S REG. NO 003052032
x. DATE OF ISSUANCE 11/02/2013 09:17:09 AM	xi. SIGNATURE OF EXAMINER OR INSPECTOR TIMOTHY WAYNE TIMBERLAKE IACRA E-SIGNED APPLICATION EA09	DATE DESIGNATION EXPIRES 11/30/2013

FAA Form 8060-4 (8-79) USE PREVIOUS EDITION   Application Number: 748708   IACRA Equivalent

vii. AIRMAN'S SIGNATURE Kim Jochl

XIV. CONDITIONS OF ISSUANCE

This is an interim certificate issued subject to the approval of the Federal Aviation Administration pending the issuance of a certificate of greater duration. It becomes void –
1. Upon the receipt of a certificate of greater duration to replace it;
2. Upon a finding by the FAA that an error has been made in its issuance;
3. Upon a finding by the FAA that is was issued illegally or as the result of fraud or mis-representation;
4. Upon the refusal or failure by the holder to accomplish a flight check by a Flight Standards Inspector if so requested; and
5. In any case, at the expiration of 120 days from date of issuance.

Wayne and I went to his office and filled out the paperwork that he had to send to Oklahoma City, where the federal aviation headquarters are located, for validation. He printed my temporary private pilot's license, and told me if I didn't receive the permanent one by February to give him a call. Oh yes, and he told me, "Congratulations!"

He quickly headed out to meet Katherine. The weather was getting mystical and eerie.

In a daze, exhibiting true blond qualities, I felt like I was walking on water to the parking lot, looked around as if it was jam-packed, spotted Katherine's old Toyota (the only car in the lot), manually unlocked the door instead of the usual remote, and got in to start the drive back to 0A9. With the weather the way it was, I was thankful to have my check ride behind me and not to be flying solo back to 0A9.

While exiting the airport road en route to I-81 South, I texted everyone—*I'm a pilot.*

My accomplishment was slowly starting to sink in. The excitement was growing. I could barely contain myself. I-81 was becoming a little busier than usual and things didn't look familiar. Katherine's car had no GPS, no compass, no atlas, and I had no clue. I was supposed to exit near Bristol, Tennessee. I exited I-81 somewhere. It was now looking completely unfamiliar. I entered what appeared to be a rural office area.

Kim, this isn't correct. I turned around. *Oh, gas station on the right. I'll ask directions. Surely everyone knows where Elizabethton, Tennessee, is.* I pulled in and parked the car.

By now I was radiating excitement. I really, really, truly had a pilot's license. *Pull yourself together, calm down. You're lost and you need to ask for directions to Elizabethton. You need to appear normal.* All I wanted to do was get out of the car, throw my hands in the air, and jump around hootin' and hollering.

But of course I didn't do that.

It was okay that I was lost. No big deal. I was on the ground. Two girls who appeared to be nice walked out of the gas station convenience store. I asked for directions to Elizabethton. They weren't real sure but took a guess. I followed their advice to get back on 81 South, go a little farther, and watch for signs for Bristol. Good enough for me. I did exactly that and eventually arrived safely at the Elizabethton airport, where my car was waiting for me.

During the schizophrenic drive back to Elizabethton, I realized I needed to call my mom. She was home. Breathless, my words and excitement tumbled out of me. Mom listened, interrupted, listened some more, interrupted again to talk about stuff unrelated to me earning my private pilot's license. Okay. I politely listened to her, but only for a few seconds, then quickly changed the subject back to me and my flying.

"Wow, Kimmie that's great! I knew you would do it. You're so smart and you've worked so hard. And just think how scared you were!" she said, probably over and over again. She always says things like that, no matter how brilliant or trivial the accomplishment is. Even if we fail, she communicates the same pride, just changing the words to "At least you tried. How many people even try? You should be real proud."

When I paused long enough to listen, she said, "You really need to calm down, though, so you don't get lost and get home safely."

"Oh, Mom, of course I'll get home safely! Don't worry." And I started talking at full speed again. I didn't dare tell her that I had already managed to get lost. How do moms always know what's going on, even if they don't?

Finally, just before she got off the phone I said, "Be sure to tell Dad, OKAY? Don't forget, tell Dad right away."

I started the day's flight with no radio communication,

avoided being hit in midair by an airplane, greased the landing in ten knots crosswind gusting to fourteen, passed a check ride, and ultimately earned my private pilot's license. But ironically, I got lost driving home. Can you believe it? I felt like one of those smart people who are only good at one thing, but terrible at everything else.

In February of 2014, my official, non-temporary, laminated pilot's license arrived in the mail from Oklahoma City. I didn't tell anybody I had received it. When I encountered each person who had gone through this experience with me, I handed them my license, let them hold it in their hands and read it.

"What's this?" they questioned.

"It's my private pilot's license!" I replied.

Each one looked up at me and smiled.

CHAPTER FOUR
Spoiled Rotten Brat

I'm a spoiled rotten brat! You'll call me that too soon enough. Keep reading.

About a month before I actually passed the oral exam and check ride, the thought of owning my own airplane crept into my head. *Kim, you don't even have your license yet. You're getting ahead of yourself and you're going to jinx everything. That's bad karma.*

Regardless, I investigated secretly. I typed "Skylane 182" into Google. Pages and pages of used 182s for sale popped right up. I was hooked, periodically checking www.controller.com for a used Skylane.

But how do I break the news to Gunther? I thought and thought about it for quite some time, until finally I got it. My idea about buying a small airplane for me was logical . . . even smart, and I came up with a good argument that I would present to Gunther at just the right time—which was sure to materialize when I least expected it.

There we were in the cockpit of 4 Echo Quebec: an experienced pilot and a beginner pilot, a husband and a wife. Lots can go wrong with this setup. But it didn't. I was the pilot and he was my passenger for the very first time. He was calm, quiet, and relaxed. His unexpected easiness made me comfortable. He was fidgety, though. By nature, Gunther's fidgety, mainly because his mind is always working. I don't think it ever takes a break, even when he sleeps. He's a uniquely driven man. Always focused on solving, even the impossible.

4 Echo Quebec was an aging, well used, but reliable student airplane. Before we got in and during my pre-flight, Gunther did his own conspicuous inspection, judging everything. I thought, *Please be discreet. Don't embarrass me in front of the Elizabethton Airport personnel. They're my pals.* He fixed the door seal, tightened the loose and sometimes visually obstructive sun visors, and securely reattached the door panels.

Sure, I was tiny bit nervous about flying with Gunther, but I was confident and focused. I flew him from the Elizabethton Airport over Watauga Lake, Beech, Sugar, and Grandfather Mountains toward Spruce Pine, and then circled back along the North Carolina / Tennessee border to Elizabethton. The trip seemed effortless, even enjoyable. Gunther often viewed the landscape, reveling in the vast beauty, and interested in identifying all that was below. Seldom is he not the pilot in command. I think he enjoyed it.

Of course, he fiddled with leaning the engine (to increase power and fuel efficiency a pilot reduces the flow of fuel into the air fuel mixture, resulting in better engine performance), scanned the instruments periodically, asked what my airspeed was, and broadened my knowledge of basic flying by explaining some of the more advanced things one doesn't typically learn during the initial stages of obtaining a private pilot's license.

After we landed, he borrowed the crew car from the Elizabethton Municipal Airport and took me to McDonald's for lunch. He was proud of me.

The winter season was upon us, and Gunther, Olivia, and I were out to dinner at the Painted Fish, a restaurant at the base of Sugar Mountain. It was a cold, raw, dreary sort of early winter evening. Without preparation or even thinking, my mouth just started with, "Gunther, I think we should buy a Cessna Skylane 182. Before you say no, think about it. Let's find an inexpensive, used, older-model Skylane that needs updating and some fixing, one that's sound but just needs us to bring it back to life. You're an A&P. You can do all the work, with my help of course. It's a buyer's market. This would be an investment, and not just an airplane for me," I rambled on with excitement.

I could see Gunther's wheels were turning. He was silent, thinking. I'd captured his attention. He loves to work on airplanes, thrives on a challenge, and I knew he would enjoy flying a 182. There was no doubt in his mind or mine that, with time, we could make money on a 182 if we found the right deal.

Olivia was all ears, but getting annoyed. She'd had enough of airplane talk. She chimed in. "Mom, don't you think you need to save your money for retirement?"

What? I thought. Did I just hear her correctly? *My twelve-year-old retirement specialist is worried about my future?* Hardly. She just wants the time, energy, and focus that I spend on airplanes to be redirected.

"Olivia, I appreciate your concern about my retirement, and more importantly that at your age you understand and value the concept of retirement. But I've been saving for retirement since I was twelve years old," I informed her.

She gave me that look that only a tween girl can give her mother and rolled her eyes.

"That's right, Olivia. I delivered the *Berkshire Eagle* news-paper every morning before seven a.m. when I was twelve years old and worked summer and weekend jobs ever since then. All of my paper route money and any other earnings went straight into the Berkshire Bank popcorn savings account, designed specifically for kids," I said.

Gunther was sensing the tension between Olivia and me, and questioned my savings initiative at such a young age as well.

"Whether you two believe me or not is irrelevant. My parents taught me how to earn and save my money at an early age, and I continue to do so," I told them both.

But back to the airplane: Gunther liked the idea; I could feel it. He made no commitments but the discussion continued in a hopeful direction.

Olivia returned to her iPad, disgusted. But I am sure she listened to every word we said.

Does my Dad like to fly? Is he afraid? I really didn't know. I was taking him to Elizabethton to fly with me for the very first time, and he seemed pretty excited about it.

When we arrived, I pre-flighted, and then we both settled into 4 Echo Quebec. I ran through the start-up procedures, firmly held the brakes, primed the engine, switched the master on, and turned the key to spark the magnetos that eventually turn the propeller.

Silence.

The engine wouldn't start. Not a sound, no hint of a spark, nothing. I was baffled and couldn't seem to identify the problem. One thing was clear, there was no power. Maybe the battery was dead. I worried: *What's my Dad thinking?* I was a little embarrassed, and worried about him being worried. *Wait a minute*, I thought. *This happened with Gunther several weeks ago when I took him out for the very first time.* I told Dad it was no big deal. I radioed Unicom and told them that I needed some assistance. Dan and Jacob came out immediately with a battery charger. They hooked it up, and in no time the engine was running, propeller spinning. They gave me the thumbs-up and unhooked the charger. I looked at Dad. He appeared skeptical, and unsure, and asked me lots of questions. I didn't know all the answers, but tried to be reassuring.

"Are you ready, Dad?" I asked.

"Yup," he said.

"Okay, here we go!" I said. "Elizabethton traffic, Skyhawk 734 Echo Quebec's taxiing to runway six," I communicated.

Just six months before, when I had taken Krista flying with John right seat, she'd said, "Kim, you really should speak with more confidence on the radio. Don't be so timid." I had been a nervous wreck back then, embarrassed to even communicate my intentions over the radio, afraid I would say something stupid.

Now, it was all second nature.

Upon reaching cruising altitude and stabilizing the airplane I said, "Dad, here's my camera. Take a picture of me."

He took a picture.

"No Dad, get a better one; lean back a little so you can get more of me. Get the instrument panel in there, and try to get outside, too," I said—like he should know better.

He did as instructed.

"Take another one. One more, take another one." Once I quit bugging him about getting me on camera, he went crazy and took picture after picture of the beauty beyond.

Later when I viewed the pictures on my computer I saw he'd gotten some really great shots. There were a few good ones of me, and one very cool shot of 4 Echo Quebec's instrument panel and runway six at the Elizabethton Airport on final. I love that picture.

Our trip was about an hour long. We flew over Cross Mountain, Shady Valley, South Holston Lake, then landed at the Virginia Highlands Airport. It was a good landing. We then took off again. This time we flew over Watauga Lake, Beech and Sugar Mountains, and circled back to Elizabethton safe and sound. Dad now truly believed that I could fly.

I'm pretty sure he liked it. He was nervous, but I sensed that he settled in and relaxed as the flight progressed. He'd fly with me again, for sure.

511

A few weeks after expressing my desire to own a Skylane, I was peeking through the window of a brick hangar at the Ashe County Airport, looking at a 1969 Cessna Skylane 182M, tail number N71511. No letters, like N734EQ, just numbers. Well, okay, there's an N. But every airplane originating in the United States begins with the letter N. That identifies which country it's from. X is Mexico, D is Germany, *OE* is Austria and so on.

On paper, the airplane looked ideal: exactly the investment and airplane we were looking for. The airframe had less than 1,000 hours and there were only 120 hours on the engine.

It was white, black, and mostly red, old and very cool looking. The airplane was long, skinny, and standing confident—something I instantly imagined myself flying. I loved it.

I turned to Gunther, who was peeking in alongside me. "Where is he?" I asked.

We were waiting for Ronnie Ray, the owner of the airplane. He was late. I paced the local surroundings, and peeked at "my" airplane again several times through the window.

The excitement was building. *This airplane is mine. I know it. It just feels right. It's old, but not cheesy. The price is reasonable, but Gunther thinks there's room to negotiate. What if it smells inside? What if it's that super bad, cornball 1960s style? Some '60s stuff is very hip, but the bad '60s is really bad, unacceptable, potentially embarrassing.*

I was getting anxious. Ronnie Ray was still not there; about a half hour had passed. Gunther called him. He was on his way, about ten minutes out. That means twenty minutes or longer anywhere in the mountains of Western North Carolina. It could be a while.

At last, he arrived. He was super nice, pleasant, overly informative. Definitely a talker, but reserved, 'cause he was sentimental about selling his baby. Ronnie opened the hangar door and gave us free rein to look around. Both Gunther and I were like horses just out of the gates at the Kentucky Derby.

We headed in separate directions to inspect the airplane. Gunther of course knew what to look for. Me, well, I just looked, admired, and slowly made my way around the exterior. I looked over the airplane as if I was conducting a preflight inspection. That's all I knew to do.

Gunther and I climbed inside the airplane. I was in the pilot's seat; he was right seat. We fiddled, looked things over, felt and touched the seats, arm rests, and door panels along with whatever else. Gunther looked at me and said, "Do you like it?"

"I really do," I said.

Ronnie locked up the hangar. We all shook hands, and Gunther said to Ronnie, "I'll be back over in the next few days to do a pre-buy inspection with Mike."

Mike is the IA DAR, a FAA Inspection Authority and Designated Airworthiness Representative. He knows his stuff. If Mike gave his thumbs-up on the airplane, we'd be buying a new/old 1969 Cessna Skylane. I was on the verge of being a spoiled rotten brat who just six months ago was still in heart attack mode whenever flying in small airplanes.

I still worried about flying, but the combination of knowledge and experience made a difference in my fear factor.

The fuel bladders were bad, and the King radios would need replacing. The transponder was an old Narco; it would need replacing as well. The headliner was old and had stains on it. Otherwise, the airplane was clean.

It was Saturday, a workday for us. Gunther left early that morning to meet Mike over at the Ashe County airport to perform the pre-buy inspection, which lasted until about three p.m. They did a thorough inspection of the airframe and engine, a compression check, opened all inspection panels, and meticulously read over the log books. Periodically throughout the day, I would tap my fingers on my desk, distracted and waiting for more news.

All was in order! Gunther made a deal, called the insurance company, and flew N71511 (511) to Elizabethton. Often traffic controllers and pilots reduce an airplane's tail number to the last three digits, particularly in heavy traffic to speed up communication, hence 511.

"I'm flying home with the airplane. Meet me in Elizabethton," Gunther said, calling me from the air in my new/old 1969 Cessna Skylane 182M.

I was so excited. I got Olivia and we drove to the Elizabethton airport. The clouds were heavy, and the air was damp and rainy; it was not a nice day to be flying.

But there it was: my airplane. Both fuel tanks were dripping fuel. I approached it slowly, almost afraid but very excited to take on every challenge that lay ahead. It was humbling. A whole new world awaited.

The three of us got into the car and drove home. (I'm sure we stopped at McDonald's along the way.)

A few days later, Gunther and I drove back to Elizabethton. The weather was still marginal, but good enough for him to fly the ailing Skylane home to the Elk River Airport, a VFR-only private airstrip nestled in the Appalachian Mountains and just five miles from our house. It's where 511 is hangared. Both arrived safely.

The next day the work began.

Reactions

How does a girl tell anyone she owns and flies her own airplane? It's an unusual possession, and the reactions from people can be unpredictable, sometimes fun. Sharing this tidbit of information extolled a wide range of emotion: excitement, shame, pride, insecurity, pleasure.

I texted Krista a picture of my new/old airplane. She was ecstatic, stunned, and happy, like it was hers. She immediately wondered when I was flying up to Washington, DC, to visit. How far I could take her, and when? She made me feel good.

I told her it would be a while. The airplane required lots of work, and I still needed to get my high-performance endorsement, which is a proficiency rating for an airplane with more than 200 horsepower. You have to get the endorsement from a certified flight instructor like John. (My airplane, 511, has 230 horsepower. 4 Echo Quebec had about 160 horsepower.) Knowing me, I wouldn't venture very far from home until I had practiced everything a gazillion times.

For Mom and Dad, the telling was an in-person thing. I wanted to get their reaction firsthand and observe how they genuinely felt about the matter. Over the phone I wouldn't have been able to read their facial expressions or see their body language. They couldn't believe it. As a matter of fact, they didn't believe it. I think Dad accepted it before Mom. Even when Mom accepted it, she still couldn't believe it.

Mom and Dad live in Lee, Massachusetts, and visit often. They bought a house close to us, but can't quite commit to a permanent move. During their Christmas visit I showed the airplane to Mom—Dad, too, but his reaction was reserved. He's reserved by nature, and contains his emotions and reasons things out for a lengthy period of time—unless he's angry. But Mom, she wears her emotions on her sleeve. (She can keep a secret though! Like every Friday night when we were young we got pizza for dinner while Dad was at work. Mom wasn't supposed to spend extra money on pizza. We had to keep that a secret.)

"Oh my Gawd," she said in her heavy Boston accent.

"Guntha, you are spoiling this kid rawtten!"

"Mom, no he's not. It's an old airplane; it needs lots of fixing," I said, which wasn't really the right thing to say. Then she worried the airplane was unsafe, but I was only trying to downplay the enormity of having my own airplane.

Just be quiet, Kim, I said to myself.

"I am nawt riding in a clunkah," was her next statement.

Oh good grief, I thought. I had to laugh. *Just take it in stride, Kim.*

Then she saw it. It's red. Lots of red.

"Wow, honey, it's red. I love the colah. Maybe I do like it. This is wondaful," she said.

My parents were digesting the fact that their daughter owned and flew her own airplane. This was heavy. And I thought soloing was tough!

I told my brother, Erich, who lives in our area with his family. He backed up a little bit, and his eyes semi-bugged out of his head. Then he broke into a big grin, and was excited and very happy for me. My older sister, Sherri, who also lives close by, was super excited, but a little nervous about the whole idea.

The reactions continue to be priceless and entertaining. Who woulda thought!

Repairs and Renovations

Gunther had his work cut out for him with rejuvenating this airplane. But he loves a challenge and I could tell he was thriving on it.

The leaking fuel tanks took priority. After all, you can't operate any type of engine without fuel. First, new heavy-duty Monarch fuel caps and new seals replaced the old ones. That didn't stop the leaks, which he thought could be a long-shot solution but fairly cheap, versus the expense and labor needed to replace the fuel bladders. Gunther got help from Ronnie, a local mechanic (who at the age of fourteen tore down a smoking 1965 Volkswagen Beetle engine and rebuilt it without a glitch—amazing people, they're everywhere!) and Chris, a young local guy who can do anything. They spent hours installing new fuel bladders and replacing all the rubber fuel lines. Chris—he's a twin like me—was vital to the job because he has long arms, necessary when installing the long-range fuel tank bladders. The intricacies of the job made it time-consuming and tedious. I heard the stories and witnessed the grease and cuts on Gunther's hands and arms, and saw the weariness in his demeanor after a hard day's work at the hangar.

Next Gunther ripped out the faded, stained headliner from the cockpit ceiling. He kicked out the old ELT (emergency locator transmitter—when you crash an airplane the ELT sends signals letting officials know where you are), both King nav/coms, the King audio controller, the King ADF (automatic directional finder), and the Narco transponder.

It was then time to reassemble all that had been kicked out and add personal touches. Gunther installed an avionics master switch, a Garmin GNS 530 WAAS, a brand new Narco nav/com, two new navigation indicators with glide slope, additional aircraft breakers, a new ELT, and a new PSE audio controller. I helped a little.

That's not all. He resealed the windows and windshield with Pro Seal, installed an Airwolf oil filter kit, replaced the nose wheel and one main wheel, removed all unnecessary antennas plus both communication antennas and one navigation antenna. He installed one new com antenna and one new GPS WAAS antenna.

The only cheesy thing in 511 was the corny, obnoxious rearview mirror located smack dab in the middle of the glare shield (on the dashboard for non-flyers). I hated it.

Mom always said, "Kimmie, you don't evah hate anything. Nevah use the word hate. You may dislike something, but you nevah hate anything."

When I was little I minded what my mother said, and kept the word hate out of my vocabulary. I still do for the most part, but I did *hate* the rearview mirror in my airplane. We kicked it out!

Lastly, Gunther placed insulation on the ceiling and with great care installed the new headliner.

The overhaul was complete. 511 is now worth a whole lot more than it was when we bought it, and not just monetarily. Gunther did all the work in between his real 24/7 job. . . . And yes, men work 24/7, just like us!

CHAPTER FIVE
Big Baby Steps

Generally during the winter months the winds at the Elk River Airport come from the west/northwest and can often be strong. That means three zero, the steep approach over and around the mountains that requires a heavy, heavy dose of courage, is the preferred runway for landing. Skill is also required, of course, along with a copilot who knows and can execute an Elk River Airport three zero approach and landing in his sleep. That's Gunther.

I had Gunther, so that was no problem; the skill to fly I had already learned and loved practicing. Courage was a little easier to acquire with the first two well in hand. But fear lingered.

During January and February, I flew 511 with Gunther as my copilot/instructor many times, practicing the pattern into the Elk River Airport. I got through nine takeoffs and landings. It was heart racing, heart pounding, heart thumping, heart everything! Nothing like getting thrown into advanced flying, and with a new/old airplane. Gunther scolded me for my failings as much as he complimented me for my skills. If I couldn't comfortably get in and out of the Elk River Airport by myself, I couldn't really do much flying. Elizabethton is tame compared to the rugged mountain landing strip at Elk River. John says if I could land on runway three zero at Elk River, I could land on an aircraft carrier.

I drew the Elk River pattern on paper, just like John taught me. This pattern isn't typical, though. The pattern altitude is more than the standard 1,000 feet above runway elevation, mountains surround the airport at varying elevations during every point of the pattern, and short final descents are obnoxiously steep at both ends. Approach speeds are always the same here or at any other airport. I studied and memorized everything: procedures, terrain, variable weather situations, and

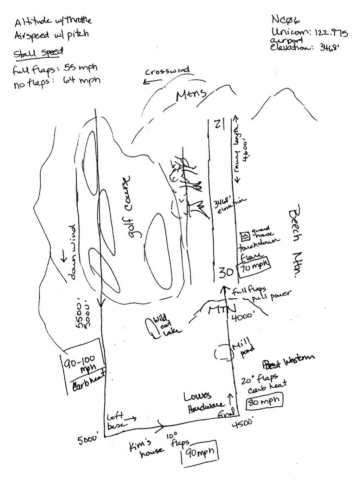

speeds. It scared me to study the pattern. Studying is one thing, but the execution is entirely different. It's not as simple as regurgitating learned or memorized information. It's real! It's physical. And eventually it had to be performed SOLO!

Every successful step pushed me to reach the next one even when fear and insecurity dominated.

High-Performance Endorsement

After earning a private pilot's license, the next logical step was to obtain a high-performance endorsement. Since 511 is a high-performance airplane, I needed to be certified to fly a high-performance airplane. I was to meet John at the Elk River Airport to begin working on the endorsement.

Flying is seldom easy for me, even at this stage. I had butterflies in my stomach and I was nervous about landing 511 at any airport. I was excited about working on maneuvers, but at the same time that nagging voice was saying, *Wouldn't it be more pleasant to go shopping?* It was a nice, calm spring day, a chilly thirty degrees. I could drive over to Johnson City and head to Barnes and Noble, watch people, look at books, and maybe even buy one. I needed a new book. I had just finished reading *Joan of Arc* by Mark Twain. A relaxing day seemed so much easier than the mental load and actual execution required to fly an airplane.

But instead of taking advantage of a leisurely day off, I dragged myself out of bed. Gunther and I arrived at the Elk River Airport at eight thirty a.m. I pre-flighted while Gunther did some last minute work on 511. John arrived at nine. We pulled the airplane out of the hangar, went through the usual checklists and briefings, then took off. 511 popped right off the runway.

On the flight over to Elizabethton, we worked on a few basic high-performance aircraft differences that were new to me. Cowl flaps: an air intake under the nose of the airplane that needs to be opened and closed at specific times during the flight to keep the engine cool. The variable pitch propeller changes the angle of the propeller, allowing for a more aerodynamic position while cruising, or greater pull when climbing. These were about the only procedural differences from 4 Echo Quebec. I was also not 100 percent confident with operating the manifold pressure correctly (it's sort of a complicated explanation, but simply stated, manifold pressure regulates power). I was hoping repetition would ease my discomfort. I flew a pattern into Elizabethton runway two four. I was uptight, but John walked me through it when necessary. The approach and landing was seamless and smooth. My smile was bigger than ever.

We pulled into the FBO (fixed base operator) to get fuel. I was reminded of what a great place the Elizabethton Airport is and how helpful, warm, and friendly the guys are. Mike, one of the Elizabethton Municipal Airport employees, asked me if I was working on my instrument rating (or IFR, a set of flight rules and regulations determined by the FAA that depends upon electronics or instruments for navigation). I said "No, just my high-performance endorsement," thinking, *One big baby step at a time for me.* Right now I was worried about landing safely at the Elk River Airport in the next hour—never mind the instrument rating! But then I realized: *They think I'm smart enough and competent enough to move on to instrument. That's flattering and encouraging.*

Once the airplane was fueled, John and I took off on runway two four. I turned and headed for Shady Valley. John had me work on fifteen-degree bank turns, and then the more challenging and dizzying forty-five-degree steep turns—both ways. I held altitude, kept the ball in the middle (that means the turn-and-bank-indicator instrument was properly centered—my turn was coordinated), maintained the forty-five-degree bank, and became dizzy. But I got it. We worked a little with the GPS. Then slow flight, which progressed into power-on stalls. I was quickly reminded that I don't like stalls and told John. He didn't care. It's unnerving, scary, and still takes me forever to get to stall speed (55 mph with the flaps fully extended, or 64 mph with no flaps). I did at least two stalls, then continued slow flight until we got to pattern position at the Elk River Airport.

I flew the Elk River Airport pattern, remembering everything Gunther had taught me during our practice sessions throughout January and February—pattern altitude 5,000 feet until the big field, turn base, line up over the mountain with the runway, pass over Three-Mile Hill at 4,500 feet, stay close to the terrain on the right, airspeed at 80-90 mph, 20-30 degrees of flaps. As soon I saw the runway numbers above the last and final hill, I pulled the power, dropped the nose, hoped the speed was still at 80 mph, and got it on the ground as soon as possible. I kept the airplane straight, flared, and touched down. Intense!

Prior to every procedural execution, I told John what I was going to do, often saying, "This is what Gunther said," "This is how Gunther told me to do it," "Gunther said to do it this way," or "Gunther says these are the speeds I have to hit," etc., etc., etc. I would then say, "Is that okay, John?"

John always agreed, and sometimes offered a supplemental suggestion. I must have been annoying.

I floated my landing more than usual. No bounce, though— just coasted slightly above runway one two, reduced power, and gently touched down. I maintained focus, keeping the airplane straight during run-out. And I was relieved, relieved, relieved.

Strangely, I couldn't function beyond the immediate task of taxiing safely off the runway. John said something, Gunther was at the departure end of runway three zero, and I ignored both of them unintentionally. Soon enough, though, I was able to take in the things around me. We taxied to the hangar and put 511 away. It was a successful day. Certainly more rewarding than a day at Barnes and Noble. But relaxing? NO!

Even though it was pretty windy at the Elk River Airport, John and I planned another high-performance training day. It was gusty, but not in a frightening way. The winds were 8 to 12 mph when they blew. I was a little nervous. John was a tiny bit too. I know because I asked him. We know Elk River (NC06) is a tough airport to land in. There is terrain up to 6,000 feet surrounding the runway, with the extra-steep descent into runway three zero. One two is the preferred runway. However, runway three zero is more appealing in the event of a missed approach. Don't plan a missed approach on one two. Get it on the ground the first time, because there's a mountain at the end of runway one two.

We back taxied (this is when you taxi on the runway instead of a taxiway, since a taxiway doesn't exist at the Elk River Airport) to runway three zero. I did the run-up and checked the winds. They were down a bit to between 4 and 8 mph. *Okay, good to go.* I changed my takeoff/rotate speed to 65 mph from the POH (pilot's operating handbook, which I read cover to cover) recommendation of 60 mph because the stall warning kept buzzing when I took off at 60 mph. I checked the POH for stall speed. It said stall speed is 64 mph. What's up with that—64 stall, 60 rotate? Why is the stall warning going off? I researched, debated, compared, and analyzed those numbers for a while. I told Gunther and John. Both had logical explanations. Nonetheless, I was uneasy about the numbers, so I decided I was going to rotate (rotate means to pull the yoke gently back during takeoff until the airplane becomes airborne while working the rudder in order to keep the airplane going forward in a straight line) at 65 mph from then on. Both agreed and said, "That's fine, Kim"—

like, *It's a good idea, but there was no reason to go through the analysis you went through!*

Weeks later, Gunther told me a couple of times during takeoff that I tended to pull the yoke too abruptly, creating a steep angle of attack; with the swirling winds at the Elk River Airport, the stall levers flap back and forth, causing the stall warning to inadvertently go off. I've since made adjustments to the way I rotate, and haven't heard a stall warning since. Yay! Problem solved.

John and I took off at 65 mph. All went well. We climbed to 6,000 feet, where it wasn't bumpy anymore. John went over the use of mixture and leaning the engine. I followed along while keeping the airplane flying. Leaning the engine was a little confusing, but I knew that with repetition I'd get that too. Next he instructed me to perform clearing turns and steep turns. When I kept my eyes outside on the horizon with periodic scanning of the instruments, I held altitude and the turn coordinated. I did it correctly during the second steep turn. On the first turn, I got sucked into watching the instruments more often than the horizon and consequently had a harder time maintaining altitude.

We worked down to slow flight: 90 mph and 30 degrees of flaps, while maintaining altitude by adjusting several controls. I really had to pay attention, because it was a lot to comprehend simultaneously. Imagine your brain doing gymnastics: that's what learning to fly is like sometimes. We did three landings into Elizabethton, one touch-and-go. The landings were okay, and I didn't have to use all my might to keep the nose up anymore. That was a good feeling. John explained it was because I was using the trim more effectively and starting to get a feel for the airplane. "The feel" is a critical tool that's challenging to learn if the teaching variables aren't right. My "feel" undoubtedly came from Gunther sharing his expertise in the air with me, John walking me patiently through maneuvers, and practice, practice, practice.

As we headed back to the Elk River Airport I was feeling confident. I have no idea why, because it's a challenging airport and it was very windy. Ten miles out, I called the Elk River Unicom; winds were 8 to 15 mph out of the northwest. That means we needed to land runway three zero: the scary approach, and the one that takes extra courage to execute. I was mentally prepared and looking forward to making it happen. We flew the pattern; I was above the last high peak on short final, about 4,500 feet. Winds were 12 mph out of the northwest. I saw the runway numbers clearly and pitched the nose down, steeply down. I needed to lose a lot of altitude in a very short distance. The runway altitude is 3,468 feet. I was dropping at about 1,700 feet per minute. It was not going to take me a minute to get to the runway. I needed to lose altitude more quickly. The nose was down and the airspeed was increasing—not good. I pulled the power. John added more flaps. We were over the runway and close to touchdown. I flared a little too soon and aggressively, but patiently let the nose ease, and we touched down a bit roughly but with plenty of runway to spare. I couldn't wait to do it better next time.

After shutdown, John said, "Well, how do you feel? Are you comfortable with the airplane?"

I talked and talked and talked. When we were out of the airplane and pushing it back into the hangar I quit rambling for a moment, at which time John quickly (before I started up again) and without expression said, "Well, I'm going to give you your high-performance endorsement."

"WHAT? Really? Okay, that's great!" I responded in a state of shock.

I hadn't expected to get the endorsement that day. I beelined it to my car to fetch my logbook and a pen so he could sign it before he had the chance to change his mind.

I hadn't even worn my purple short-sleeved shirt. (See, I told you I'm not superstitious!) I tried to call Gunther. No answer, so I texted him as well as Krista.

The Other Side of Flying

Early one spring day, Gunther had flown to the Tri-Cities Airport in the Cheyenne to get some fuel for our trip to Eagle, Colorado, the next day, so he knew what the conditions were like—he thought.

Shortly after he returned, he and I took off in 511 to do some pattern practice at Elk River. Upon takeoff, the winds were reported calm. But we knew they were swirling up to 14 knots. Gunther knew it was somewhat bumpy up above.

We took off from runway three zero, flew the pattern for landing on runway one two. We were on crosswind, over Banner Elk, just above the Lowe's Hardware. The wind was pushing me close to the runway. I was uptight, but had to stay focused and compensate. Out of nowhere, we hit a pocket of turbulence. Gunther did not have his seat belt snug, and the unexpected jolt banged his head against the roof and knocked his headset off his head. Ouch! The airplane dropped, and then smashed back to forward flight.

I was strapped in tightly, but I felt the hard jolt too. After that drop out of the sky—holy cow!—my focus and determination were razor sharp.

Turbulent weather persisted, shaking us up and down, back and forth. Gunther was dizzy. I wasn't sure if he was okay.

"Are you okay?" I asked.

No response.

Again, I asked more urgently, "Are you okay?"

He responded slowly, "Yeah, I'm okay." I kept flying the airplane, relieved to know he was still with me.

I knew he was okay when he began to give me instruction again.

I didn't dare tell him, *I don't want to fly anymore. Take the controls!* because I knew he wouldn't, and he wouldn't like that sort of behavior. So I kept on, determined to land safely. The thought of the wind and turbulence smashing us into Beech Mountain crossed my mind. Without hesitation I thought, *That won't happen.* I also wouldn't breathe a word to him about the fact that my left leg was shaking uncontrollably, to the point that it didn't function. My head kept saying, *Overcome it, Kim, overcome it. You need to use the left pedal for the rest of the trip.* I forced my brain to take over and get control of things. It did. (Later, I realized that I was working the left rudder with all my might just to keep the ball in the middle and the airplane going straight. As a result, my muscles were cramping from fatigue.)

Just before base, after the heavy turbulence, Gunther finally asked me if I was okay.

I quickly and confidently said, "Yes. I'm good. I got this."

Despite shaking from head to toe, I maintained that crazy razor-sharp focus, and we landed fine. Gunther talked me through the approach and never touched the controls. Just after touchdown, I had to work hard to keep the airplane straight on the runway because the winds were gusting with incredible speed and strength. Once we landed and all was okay, Gunther took inventory of himself, realized the airplane might have a dent in the ceiling, and noted that his head had a bump on it.

I was a statue: I didn't talk, didn't push the brakes, I just let the airplane roll out and stared straight into space. *We're okay. I'm okay,* I thought, in shock. Gunther was talking, complimenting me, giving me instructions. I didn't have the composure to talk back, but I *tried* to listen.

As I taxied back to the hangar, I was feeling a little better and told Gunther everything I hadn't told him in the air about how hard it was to control the airplane. He was amazed, but more importantly so excited that I had command and did things right, and even landed well.

Sigh. Do other pilots have these types of emo⁴ⁱonal and dramatic experiences, or am I just different?

Maintenance

Airplanes require endless amounts of attention and tender love and care. Gunther and I know that and enjoy the work and challenge.

One Saturday we changed the worn-out main-wheel left tire. The right main tire was still good. It took a couple of hours. I cleaned lots of parts, lubricated bearings, unscrewed screws, screwed hubcaps and wheel fairings, looked up the tire's air pressure in the Pilot's Operating Handbook, pulled the tube from the tire, reinserted the old tube into the new tire, measured the brake disc to ensure it was still good—yup, it's still good—lowered the jack (the airplane almost fell on me—just kidding), while Gunther did lots and lots of other equally important things.

I don't have a pink maintenance jumpsuit or pink tools. I do wear gloves and clean up anything whenever Gunther lets me.

It was physically tough work. Muscles and joints are on a concrete floor for hours bending, standing, sitting, and stuck in uncomfortable positions. It makes a body stiff. The work is slow; things took a while to complete because I had to find the right tools, analyze parts, clean parts, ensure tools were clean, replace worn parts, and unexpected snags always appeared, like the wheel pin acting up. It was a super-tight fit. The old one needed replacing. It must have taken fifteen minutes to properly line the pin up and squeeze it in. The work was tedious and required a healthy dose of patience as well as a little swearing.

We finished the job. Gunther felt good. I was glad to move on to a higher-paced activity, like running.

"Don't you feel good, Kim, working on your own airplane? An airplane is like a dog: you pay attention to it, give it some TLC, and it knows. It's gonna fly better now. You'll see," Gunther said.

In a few weeks, I'd be assisting with the 511's oil change, and immediately following that was the scheduled annual inspection. I wondered what I'd be assisting with then. Until that time, I knew there were lots of things Gunther and I would fiddle with, fix, and upgrade on my airplane. He likes it when I help.

Still learning. Practice, practice, practice.

It takes time to get used to a new airplane—for me anyway. I'd been flying with Gunther and John for three days straight. Gunther and I flew to the Tri-Cities Airport, the TRSA-controlled airspace that was still a big challenge for me, because there was lots to do and all needed to be done simultaneously. The worst part was my landing, or lack thereof! Gunther actually had to take the controls and touch down. I couldn't get the airplane's longitudinal axis to line up with the runway centerline. Not good, but that's why I was still flying with someone.

Gunther and I flew again the next day, this time to KVJI. On the trip over, everything went well. I executed procedures properly, landed fine, and then headed back to the Elk River Airport. But a horrible landing. Gunther again took control of the airplane at touchdown. I was so disappointed. But I knew I had to keep practicing. He made me go again. We did another pattern at the Elk River Airport. I was apprehensive and scared, but refocused. Somehow I pulled it together and landed just fine.

Always try again. Especially when someone you trust believes in you.

I'd been working for the past few weeks on the checklists for my Skylane. There are several checklists that are all necessary and important. There are checklists for preflight inspection, passenger briefing, before start, starting engine, after-start, taxi, before takeoff, normal takeoff, short field takeoff, en-route climb, cruise, descent, pre-landing, go around (in case of a missed approach—I've done my fair share of these!), after-landing, parking, and securing the aircraft.

Before I had my license, I referred to them all the time prior to executing each operation. They provided security and made me feel comfortable. It was a lot of information to attain all at once. Now I performed the operation, then reviewed the checklist to ensure I had covered every procedure. It had become routine and was now easily retrieved from memory.

I laminated the lists, brought them to Staples, and had them spiral bound for easy use. I made two sets, one for me and one for my copilot, whoever that may be. Mine is always clipped to my yoke. I also found a functional, nontraditional clear plastic tool box at Staples for the Skylane. It's totally hip and has plenty of room for my tools and extra oil rags. It fits perfectly under the backseat of the Skylane. I continue to fill it proudly with every new tool I acquire.

I was determined to feel the same level of comfort in my 511 as I'd felt in 4 Echo Quebec. That would take time, practice, and repetition. John had come over to the Elk River Airport a couple more times to help me, and we worked on takeoffs and landings, slow flight, stalls, emergency engine-out procedures, leaning the engine, and ground reference maneuvers. That's the drill that makes me feel like a Bond girl. Instead of following that back country road in Virginia, I followed the South Holston River. I descended to about 1,000 feet AGL (above ground level, as opposed to MSL—mean sea level) and meandered the path of the river.

Practicing the simulated emergency engine failure maneuver was exciting and rewarding again. I pulled the power slowly until there wasn't any more, then worked the controls to maintain level flight, first adjusting the trim tab on the elevators to fix the pitch. Next, I pulled the carburetor heat knob to ensure the engine didn't freeze up, lowered some flaps, kept the ball in the middle with the rudder, and held the yoke when necessary to maintain 81 mph; all the while looking for a suitable place to make an emergency landing. Eighty-one miles per hour is a critical number for me to remember, or at least have noted on the checklist, because it's the Skylane's best glide rate. It's amazing how long we were able to maintain altitude and the distance we traveled before the airplane didn't really want to fly anymore. We were able to glide over the heavily forested mountain range into the valley with plenty of time to spare and locate several suitable plots of long, level surfaced fields of farmland.

About 3,000 feet above ground, I executed procedures to abort the emergency landing and got the airplane safely flying with engine power. That was great—such a rush. It's comforting to know that when an engine fails (and there is just the one engine on 511!), there's time and procedures to ensure everyone's safety.

Junkyard

Gunther and I took Ari, my six-year-old niece, and Krista, to the Ashe County Airport (KGEV) in Jefferson, North Carolina, to get fuel. One hundred low-lead is $4.95 a gallon. That's what my Skylane drinks. Fuel at all of the other local airports at the time was well above $5 per gallon, so I saved about 50 bucks.

The flight over and back went well. I executed a good landing at Ashe County Airport. But on short final at NC06 (Elk River Airport) the stall warning went off. The airplane was sinking fast and the wind was swirling. Winds often swirl at the Elk River Airport. We hit some type of air pocket just above the junkyard on short final. I increased power and pitched the nose up very gently on instinct. Fortunately, everything came together and although we landed a bit rough and bounced, I added a little power, landed again after the stall warning went off a second time, and stopped within the first third of runway one two. Gunther was VERY proud of me. But this is the funny part: after he said he was proud of me, he said he was really proud of himself because he didn't tell me what to do!

When the stall warning went off, Ari asked her mom, "Who is Aunt Kimmie beeping at?"

Krista said, "The ducks," which were indeed flying in front of the airplane. Of course I had no idea there were ducks flying by. I was focused on landing. (Way to go, Krista, for making light of the situation and ensuring little Ari had no idea that the stall warning is not a good noise to hear, ever.)

Bounced and Bounced All the Way Down the Runway

Olivia went flying with me for the very first time, only because staying home was more boring. She compared flying in my airplane to riding in a tuna can. With Gunther, Olivia and I flew to KTRI, controlled airspace, then back to NC06, and landed on runway three zero. It was an awful, horrible, and somewhat scary landing because we were too fast, too high, and the wind and bumps didn't provide any reprieve.

Later, I asked Olivia if she was scared, and she said "No, but I was nervous because you bounced and bounced and bounced all the way down the runway."

Gunther couldn't understand why he had allowed such a horrifying and incorrect approach and touchdown. I should have gone around and executed a missed approach. He beat himself up for hours about not insisting that I go around. He even brought it up again the next day.

I knew the next time I would get it right, and that all the analyzing and stress wasn't necessary. It's all about the numbers. If my speeds during the approach pattern are correct, everything will be okay, in any circumstance. That's what Gunther *always* tells me, over and over again. That's all I need to know! It's all about the numbers. I'll keep practicing—with someone by my side of course. It'll work out in due time and I *will* get it right. It's just going to take practice. I moved on.

Oil Change

I helped change the oil in the Skylane. First I taxied 511 from its hangar to our hangar (I call it the working hangar, because that's where we keep all the tools for maintenance) on the three zero end of the runway. Gunther told me to do a run-up because it would cycle the oil and help with the oil change.

Once I got my surgical gloves on and was equipped with a screwdriver, Gunther, Dad (who's a machinist by trade and wanted to help), and I removed the cowling. Gunther took care of the cowl flaps and, after a bit of jiggling, unhooking, and additional unscrewing, along with some swearing, the cowling made it off the engine and we placed it gently on the hangar floor. I'm sure I was a big help, unscrewing every screw.

By this time Ronnie, the world's most talented mechanic (Remember? I told you about him.), and Junior showed up to help us. Ronnie released the oil plug while I ensured the drain hose emptied the oil into the pan. With the cowling off, I attempted to learn firsthand about my engine. It takes ten quarts of W100 aviation oil; nine quarts for the engine and one quart for the new oil filter Gunther was going to install because my model Skylane didn't have one. It's a six-cylinder continental engine. It has two magnetos and two spark plug cables for each of the six cylinders. I identified the exhaust, the carburetor, the oil pan, and the cables that are attached to the spark plugs. I envisioned the oil lubricating the moving piston within the cylinders. What about the fuel? Where does that fit in? The annual inspection was coming up soon, so I thought I'd just nosey myself into that job to find out more.

But clearly the guys had this under control. I was getting in the way and sensed that I was asking too many questions. They didn't *need* me anymore, and they weren't contributing to my learning. It was then that I realized that changing the oil in 511 wasn't going to be my task because it was complicated, time-consuming, and needed people to be involved who knew what they were doing. It was time for me to go back to my office, get some work done, and get out of their hair.

Scaredy Cat

The sun was shining bright over the North Carolina high country and beyond the horizon. It was a great day to take Mom flying with me for the very first time. She's a scaredy cat, more frightened than I am to fly. But you know that when your daughter earns her private pilot's license, you need to put your fear aside and trust that everything will be okay. She did. Hooray, Mom!

"Mom, you and Dad meet us at the airport at 10:15 a.m. and we'll go flying," I told her the night before.

"O-o-kay, honey," she said with a stutter. The fear in her voice was reminiscent of Piglet from *Winnie-the-Pooh*. I bet she wished the day had never come.

Just before my parents arrived, I pre-flighted while Gunther took care of a few other details. Dad helped move the 511 out of the hangar. We all loaded in. I went through all of my checklists.

Not surprisingly, we encountered a few hiccups. The radios weren't 100 percent, the airplane key was missing, and we forgot to reinsert the data card into the GPS. Challenges aren't unusual to most pilots. A calm head and focused thinking tend to solve just about any deviation from the expected routine, and often we can simply just go on. For example, we didn't need the GPS. I had my iPad that contained the flight route and all the other necessary information. But we did need the airplane key, which turned out to be in Gunther's pocket. And the radios? Well, they'd work 100 percent someday.

Still on the ground and without turning back to see Mom's expression, I could feel she was trembling uncontrollably in the back seat. I knew from experience that the longer the period of time the pilot spends fiddling with things, the more uncertain frightened passengers become. But I also knew that it helps when the pilot expresses confidence while professionally and diligently working to solve the problems.

Gunther and Dad were reassuring Mom that everything was okay. Plus, she held Dad's hand tight.

Before we took off, Mom told me that Krista had informed her that flying with me was like driving in a Volkswagen Bug, except you are in the air. Okay, whatever! Mom liked that. She loves Volkswagen Bugs and would like to have a bright red one someday. When she and Dad were young they had a super cool black VW Bug. We heard lots of adorable stories about that little car over the years.

I briefed Mom and Dad prior to departure, letting them know that just after takeoff we would head to KVJI at 6,500 feet, land, take off again, and return to the Elk River Airport.

Mom again stuttered with fear, "We're going to land and then take off AGAIN?"

"Yes, Mom that's the plan," I said professionally and without emotion, ignoring her fear but taking notice.

At last, we took off from runway three zero. When I had flown with John and Daniel the previous fall in EQ, it had taken forever to get off the ground at 0A9 because they're heavy. Well, the same thing happened with my parents, only this time I was at Elk River, an airport surrounded by steep mountains. There's no room for procrastination. I was a little nervous and heard my skeptical voice say, *It's taking a long time to get airborne.* But the Skylane, equipped with 230 horsepower, got us swiftly high above the ground as soon as we reached liftoff.

Once we leveled out at cruising altitude, Gunther switched over to the KVJI AWOS. Winds were 290 at 8 gusting to 18 mph. Eeek, Mom was not going to like that! We flew on, discussing whether or not to land at the Virginia Highlands Airport. Mom was already scared just flying. If we descended, it would be bumpy and the landing might not be perfect. Gunther recommended we continue flying, but locally, and then head back to NC06. I agreed. I glanced at Mom and noticed that she briefly and quickly looked outside as if any movements she made might cause us to plummet to the ground. Nonetheless, she was doing very well despite her fear, with no visible shaking or sudden outbursts. Gunther let my parents know that we were heading back and wouldn't be landing in KVJI. Mom was relieved, and Dad was too. He wasn't scared, just glad that we were accommodating Mom.

Thankfully, the winds were calm at the Elk River Airport. The pressure was on, though. My last landing at the Elk River Airport had been, at best, horrible. Plus, I had my parents as passengers. Of course I wanted to do it right, and assure them that I was a good pilot. *It doesn't matter who my passengers are or whether I have passengers; I can land this airplane right.*

Approach was by the numbers all the way. I touched down within the first third of the runway; greased it in on the mains, and then the nose wheel gently hugged the runway! How's that for coming through?! Thank goodness I had an inner voice that reassured me. And I listened.

Gunther was overjoyed. Proud of me, but more proud of himself because he didn't say a thing, once again. He almost did, though. Just as his voice was about to give me instruction on short final, I executed whatever he was thinking. He kept quiet the entire way in until . . . immediately after landing. Then he just kept complimenting me, technical jargon after technical jargon, compliment after compliment. He said things like "Perfect approach angle, flap speed was right, carb heat was appropriately managed, touchdown was straight down the runway centerline, and a great two-pointer. The entire approach from the beginning to end was executed flawlessly." *Very sweet*, I thought. In stride, I absorbed it all nonchalantly.

But Mom, how's she doing? I sensed that she was relieved to be firmly planted on the ground. She couldn't wait to get out. "That was great, Kimmie! I am very proud of you. Now I can cross that off my bucket list," she said as she pulled herself out of the backseat, clearly eager to exit the airplane.

This was Dad's second time flying with me, and he seemed to enjoy it. Of course with Mom along, he had to appear cool as a cucumber.

Failure

On a good weather day, I decided I could solo the Skylane into Elk River.

Flying into Elk River isn't easy. That's why I asked John if he would spend a few hours just flying the Elk River pattern over and over with me until he felt comfortable with me soloing.

We met at eight thirty a.m. The weather was blue sky, with a few clouds up high, and calm winds—or so it appeared. The wind sock, flags, and weather reports were all positive—nothing I couldn't handle, and certainly nothing I hadn't already experienced at the Elk River Airport with a copilot along.

I took off with John right seat on runway three zero. Reported winds were from the southeast at 5 mph. As soon as we got in the air, though, the ride was very choppy. I climbed to 5,000 feet, flew upwind around to downwind for runway one two. The chop and turbulence continued. I felt the wind pushing us downwind fairly strongly. I reached the field, which is my marker to turn base. The air felt unusually unstable. I turned for final, and all was good in terms of airspeed, altitude, flaps were down, carb heat was out. I was lining up above Three-Mile Hill, descending to 4,200 feet. But the weather variables and conditions were beating my airplane all over the place: turbulence was shuffling us up, down, and sideways. The wind had changed direction several times and was swirling on top of that. I didn't know what to do. I was shaken and startled by the unforgiving roughness. The airplane didn't seem to react the way it was supposed to. Maybe because I wasn't adjusting the controls properly? Whatever the cause, I gave up.

On short final I gave up and told John, "I can't manage the airplane, you need to land this thing."

Clearly, since I'm writing this, we didn't crash: John took control and landed. I was clutching the dashboard with my left hand and my seat with my right hand, and saw that John had to work very, very hard to land as well as he did. It was rough: bouncing, swerving, and tilting. The weather was relentless. It didn't let up, not even for John.

We decided to call it a day. I was disappointed. I didn't physically hang my head, but that's how I felt. John didn't seem too affected by the situation or the conditions. As far as he was concerned, it was just another day of flight training and an additional experience under my belt. As far as I was concerned? Failure! I was a complete failure. I had no more thoughts of soloing anytime soon into Elk River.

Mentally I went back and forth trying to understand my behavior. *Why did I give up? I've NEVER given up and handed controls over to John or Gunther, ever. I need to become proficient landing at the Elk River Airport. It's where my airplane is hangared and five minutes from home.* I was looking forward to the next opportunity to fly. In the meantime, I knew I'd keep beating myself up for this one.

CHAPTER SIX
Aeronautical Engineer

The FAA requires periodic inspections on every airplane—that's a good thing, since unmaintained airplanes can injure and even kill lots of people! Every type of airplane has different requirements and various ways to complete the exploratory surgery. Mike, the FAA Inspection Authority (IA), Gunther, the FAA certified A&P, and I, the pilot, performed the annual inspection on 511. Mike was the authority, though.

Guess what I did? Unscrewed screws with the battery-operated DeWalt drill. Yes, I know it sounds like I was just a helper. I began to work with a smile on my face and interest in my demeanor, but thinking, *Unscrewing screws!?* I had already mastered that task when I assisted with the oil change.

Nonetheless, I was determined to know inside and out as much as possible about my airplane, even if it required using a screwdriver over and over again. While removing the metal plate from the tail wing, I discovered a cable, essentially a pulley system that moves the rudder. *Hmmm, this is interesting!* I was feeling, touching, seeing, and learning firsthand the inner workings of my 511.

Next, I unscrewed the inspection plates from beneath the main wings. Underneath those plates lived the aileron cables. When I move the yoke back and forth from the flight deck (I read in one of my flying magazines that it's socially incorrect to call the flight deck the cockpit. Whatever!), the ailerons move the airplane to the left and right around its longitudinal axis. I accidentally let one of the inspection plates fall to the ground. Gunther heard the clank and quickly cautioned me about my clumsiness. When it comes to the airplane, he is super particular, meticulous. I wasn't bothered by his reaction, just thankful. It's okay with me if every airplane mechanic has a disciplined and unforgiving demeanor. After all, it's about people's lives.

After unscrewing each inspection plate, I looked inside to see what there was to discover. Most often it was a cable or two. Sometimes it was hollow. Once I located a bunch of coated wires. But the big find was a motor!

"Gunther, take a look at this. Is that a baby motor in there?" I asked as though I had found a treasure.

Unimpressed, he said, "Yes, that's the motor that operates the wing flaps."

"Oh, wow," I said.

"Go ahead and let the flaps down," Gunther instructed.

I turned on the master switch, located on the lower right-hand side of the instrument panel, and then dropped the flaps lever. Down came the wing flaps. The motor was doing its job. I could see the mechanical operation of the wing flaps. Wing flaps increase drag, which slows the airplane in flight, but also increases lift. Throughout the approach to land, increments of flaps are let down, allowing for a more stable, controlled, and comfortable landing experience.

Hidden behind the wing flaps but exposed since I lowered the flaps, lay a few more inspection plates. I unscrewed those plates and examined inside. Gunther sprayed CorrosionX into each of the gazillion holes, and then we screwed the plates back on.

To test the airworthiness of the engine, we labored through a compression check. I pulled 511 out of the hangar and started her up. Once the engine was warm and purring like a cat (I hate cats. Okay, Mom, *dislike*), I performed the usual run-up: magneto check, carburetor heat check, and manifold pressure check. Then I held the brakes with all my strength while the engine sprinted at full power for about fifteen seconds. She revved loud and strong, shuttered and wiggled, tried to inch forward, but I kept a firm hold. I pulled the power back, secured the airplane, and returned 511 to the hangar. In the hangar she went, primed, lubricated, and ready for another phase of the required annual examination.

Once the awkward and cumbersome chore of removing the cowling from the engine was complete, Gunther detached the upper spark plugs from each of the engine's six cylinders. Then he connected the compression test gauges to the spark plug opening. I attached the compressor hose to the other end of the compression test gauges and turned on the air while he firmly held the propeller. Eighty PSI (pounds per square inch) of air rocketed into the cylinder. The comparison gauge needs to read 65 PSI or above. If not, there may be a leak in the cylinder, in which case the integrity of the cylinder could be compromised, resulting in possible engine failure. A gloomy consequence. The right-side cylinders measured 74, 72, and 70. Check! Cylinders one, three, and five measured 74, 70 and 66. Check!

I continued to be a busybody while sweat dripped from Gunther's forehead. He took a seat on the cluttered wooden box and began to research the spark plugs' "gap." The gap is the permitted space between the electrode and the ground electrode, where the spark needs to jump in order to fire the gas mixture and explode. That runs the engine.

"What are you doing?" I asked.

"I'm sitting for a moment," he replied.

"Don't sit on that dirty, messy box," I said.

"I need to bring one of my chairs over here to sit on," he responded.

"No! Please don't bring one of your old, crummy chairs into my hangar," I said.

I couldn't wait to shop for some inviting chairs, and maybe a desk, too, to put in 511's hangar, because who says airplane hangars can't have style and panache?

Gunther had no choice but to sit on that crummy box. I sat in the airplane. We both put on our research caps. He checked the POH (Pilot's Operating Handbook, in case you forgot) and the Cessna 182M maintenance manual. I skimmed the index and arbitrary pages of the parts catalog. Nothing. Couldn't find the gap measurement. We googled it—information was at our fingertips: fifteen to nineteen thousandths of an inch is the magic range for 511. Gunther unratcheted the remaining six plugs from the lower end of the cylinders. A few of 511's plugs measured twenty thousandths of an inch. No big deal. He adjusted the gap to the passable range, cleaned the plugs with a wire brush, and blew the crud out with the shop air from the compressor. Anti-seize paste was applied to prevent the plugs from getting stuck the next time they're removed. To avoid rapid deterioration, the top plugs were screwed into the lower positions, and the lower plugs were screwed into the top positions of each cylinder. Finally all twelve spark plugs were tightly torqued at 300 inch-pounds.

Careful and methodical flashlight inspections occur constantly during routine maintenance and annual inspections. "A-ha, I've spotted an oil leak," Gunther said.

Those pesky oil leaks, I thought. "Where?" I asked.

"Don't worry about it, Kim," Gunther said.

"What? Of course I'm going to worry about it," I politely snapped. I took the flashlight and beamed its spotlight into the cracks and crevices of the engine. "I don't see any oil, Gunther. Tell me specifically where it is," I said.

Somewhat impatiently, he walked to the left side of the engine, pointed with his flashlight, and said, "There."

"Oh, I see. Why's it leaking? What's the name of that part? Where does it go? Is it a problem? What are the consequences?" I asked.

"It's the oil line to the temperature gauge," Gunther replied while studiously returning to the rolling tool chest.

Unrelentingly, I asked every naive question that popped into my head, tracing the black rubber-coated oil line with my flashlight to its origin: the back side of the instrument panel! "Hmmm, I get it. The oil comes from the cylinder, passes through the black tube, and registers on the oil temperature sensor located on the upper right side of the instrument panel. Right, Gunther?" I asked.

"Yes, Kim," he said.

During every engine start-up, one of the tasks is to monitor the oil temperature gauge. If the instrument reads within the green zone, I'm one step closer to a safe flight. If not, I know the engine is not cooling or heating properly. A red flag. But, and this is a big but, it is possible the instrument needle is simply stuck. A firm tap on the device's glass window is often the solution and produces an audible sigh of relief from me.

However, further inspection indicated that the origin of the leak could possibly be the oil cooler gasket located just above the oil temperature line. The drip pan went back under the airplane's nose. We washed the oil temperature and oil cooler components and the surrounding area with Varsol, an industrial degreaser. The ever-useful air compressor blew away any excess water. A magic potion called developer was sprayed generously around the investigation zone to aid in identifying the precise location of the leak. Half-naked and a little worn out, 511 remained positive while I pulled her from the hangar once again. I entered the cabin and started the engine. The juices flowed through the airplane's cardiovascular system, warming, cooling and lubricating. I went through the standard run-up again, pulled the power back, secured the airplane and exited 511. Gunther anxiously explored the two points of contention. I came around to assist. I leaned my head in, rotated it upside down, switched my eyes back and forth over the oil cooler and oil temperature probe, and then offered my opinion.

Ignoring and working around me, Gunther said, "Yup, it's the oil cooler gasket. Do you see the drippings coming from the spacer?"

"Yup, I see it," I said, while running my rubber-glove-coated finger along the liquid to verify that it was indeed wet. "You're right, Gunther. That looks like the source of the problem," I agreed.

"Push the airplane back into the hangar, Kim," Gunther instructed.

I'm just kidding. He didn't say that.

Together, we maneuvered 511 back into her soon-to-be-cozy hangar. With the socket wrench, Gunther removed five screws and three studs from the oil cooler. I placed the drip pan back under the nose, which was a good thing, 'cause loads of oil came streaming from the cooler once it was detached from the engine case. Every loose part—screws, washers, gaskets—were placed in a Tupperware container for safekeeping. The gasket between the mounting block and the case was also dried out and rigid. Gunther scraped the goop and gunk build-up coated on the engine case and cleaned everything else. He stuffed rags into both engine case galley holes to prevent additional oil from leaking and dirt or particles from entering the engine.

"Kim, look here," Gunther said, holding the oil cooler and motioning with his hand. "The oil circulates through the cooler, cools, and then returns to the engine. Very important," he explained, like the doctor had long ago when I underwent my first knee surgery.

I glanced down into the oil pan beneath 511's nose, and adjacent to our feet pools of oil lay placid. "Looks like we'll have to add at least a quart of oil," I said.

"At least," Gunther responded. "The puzzle of working on 511 is stimulating and gratifying. Don't you agree?" Gunther asked.

"Um, yeah. In many ways it is," I said. But I couldn't help but think that this is an intense, laborious, time-consuming, physically and intellectually demanding way of experiencing gratification. The consequences of getting something wrong are substantial, severe. Lots of responsibility comes with this sort of work. There's gratification in mixing a bunch of baking ingredients together, popping them into the oven, and voilá: cupcakes! A few variations and I've got any type of cupcake my heart desires. Pleasure! Without the intensity of responsibility. However, I've now come to appreciate and crave both forms of stimulation and gratification. Now, if I can just get Gunther to bake a batch of chocolate cupcakes with coffee cream filling, he'll be complete too.

I took a pass at reassembling the oil cooler. Gunther managed to put it back together without me.

As we dug deeper, Mike, the FAA Inspection Authority (IA), noticed the augmenter tube in the muffler was broken. I didn't know what that was. "It's the metal cone inside the muffler that contains the exhaust and safely shoots it into the atmosphere. A broken tube can cause back pressure and loss of power. Additionally, a cracked muffler will leak carbon monoxide into the heat exchanger, through the heater hose, and into the cabin. The passengers and pilot slowly fall asleep and die," he explained.

Holy crap, I thought.

After all of the mechanical work I had done I didn't think of myself as just a helper anymore! I now considered myself an aeronautical engineer!

Gunther replaced the muffler. That job turned into a long, strenuous day, a good six hours, I'd say. Sometimes the disassembling, refitting, readjusting, lubricating, and reassembling of machinery turns out to take a bit longer than initially thought. My new muffler looked real pretty, though.

"Kim, you've heard about a ramp check, right?" Mike asked.

"Oh, of course. That's when the FAA without warning or notice has the right to poke and prod around in my airplane, and ask to see my pilot's license along with a photo ID," I replied.

"They won't do much to get their hands dirty. But they will ask to see your airworthiness certificate, radio registration, the POH and the weight and balance. They'll probably check the model plate under the stabilizer/aileron," he said as he pointed to it with his black mini flashlight. "Back in the '70s, the Department of Transportation required the FAA to put those plates on every airplane. It was supposed to eradicate the transportation of illegal drugs," he said.

"Oh boy," I replied.

"Kim, come over here. I need you to hold the flashlight," Gunther requested.

He was installing soundproofing insulation on the ceiling. When holding the flashlight became obsolete, he suggested I pick up the aluminum backing tape and any other scrap of material scattered within the airplane or around the hangar. The newly self-appointed aeronautical engineer was back to being just a helper, picking up trash.

The annual inspection was complete. Mike and Gunther did everything I didn't do. Gunther finished installing the headliner and I vacuumed the interior. Washing and polishing the exterior was my next chore.

Redemption

It had been ten days since my last flight, which I'd dubbed "the failure flight." The flight when I just gave up and handed the controls over to John. More like *insisted* he take over. So I was a little nervous getting back in the saddle, but I'd also been anxious to get back in the air and do it right. I knew I could. Redemption is all about proving to myself that I can succeed. Every flight is new; each has its own unique challenges and rewards. The variables are never the same.

At seven thirty a.m. the winds were calm, the sky was blue, and the air temperature was in the low 50s. 511 came off the ground quick and strong. Gunther was sitting next to me, right seat in the airplane, and instructed me to go to Elizabethton, land, taxi, take off and fly back to the Elk River Airport.

Hmm. Who's the pilot-in-command here? I thought. That voice in my head said, *Kim, he knows what he's doing. Do as you're told without question.* Okay, fine. I swiftly remembered that my last flight was an epic failure. I was obedient and performed as I was told without question or speaking. I greased the landing at Elizabethton and super greased the landing at Elk River. I had performed successfully. "That feeling" was the reward.

Bath time

I'm proud of my airplane. And even more proud every time I get to do work on it myself. But this time it was hard work. 511 had its first bath since I became its mom back in November. What I thought would be a forty-five-minute job took two hours. It's not quite as simple as giving your newborn baby a wash in the tub.

A stepladder, a bucket of soapy water, a scrub brush with a very long stem, some special spray to get the grease from the exhaust off the belly of the airplane, a green garden hose, and my 9-foot-high, 25-foot-long, and 36-foot-wingspanned airplane were all waiting eagerly on the pavement in the warm sun for me. *Okay, this will be fun,* I thought. Not even ten minutes later, I was sweating and my arms were sore. I drudged on, scrubbing the entire surface, starting with the nose and moving systematically over the top and sides of the fuselage until I reached the tail. I turned back to cover the airplane's elevator (Located at the rear of the airplane. The elevator controls the up and down movement of the airplane) and underside. All I had left were the wings and the windows. I got used to the fatigue, but rested when necessary.

Ronnie, who was working with Gunther on the Cheyenne in the hangar's pleasant protection from the sun, walked by and said, "Looking good!"

"Thank you."

Gunther added, "Looking good was never your problem." Of course, Ronnie meant the airplane. I love having guys around!

An hour or so into the job, tired, sweating, hungry, and on top of the ladder scrubbing the right wing, I said to Gunther, who was hard at work himself, "Now's a good time to take a picture of me."

"Kim, I'm busy. I don't have time to take a picture of you. Plus, I have gloves on. I'm not taking them off to take a picture of you," he said.

That's mean, I thought.

I was getting a picture with or without him. I supposed I would have to set up the self-timer. *Darn, I don't have my camera with me, only my cell phone.* I began the guilt trip on him.

It worked. He relented, but the effort was pathetic. He used his cell phone, but didn't even give me fair warning or tell me to look.

It's unattractive enough to be sweaty, dirty, wet and on top of a ladder. I needed a few moments, not long, to tidy up; sweep my hair out of my face, pull my shirt tail down. You know, those simple kinds of things.

I jumped down from the ladder, took my surgical gloves off, scurried to the rolling tool chest next to Gunther, grabbed my cell phone, and asked him nicely but firmly to please take a few nice pictures of me. He did.

The pictures came out okaaay. The point was captured. I sent the photo to Mom, Krista and a few others with the caption, *Not always a spoiled, rotten brat.*

Guess what? Krista plastered me all over Facebook, *AGAIN!* I'm one of those few, rare human beings who's not on Facebook and have absolutely no interest in being there for any reason. But I wouldn't be completely honest if I didn't tell you that I did ask Krista who "liked" the photo.

Washing and rinsing the upper and lower surface of the wings took a long time. I got it done and finished with the windows and windshield. It still needed polishing, the whole thing! That would be another day. I pushed 511 back into its hangar, and before shutting the hangar door my Skylane thanked me. I left feeling pretty good. Worn out and wet, but pretty good.

Spitball

I wore my purple shirt, knowing that I would solo my new/old airplane, 511, at Elizabethton. Puffy, scattered, beautiful clouds filled the sky around the Elk River Airport to the east and west at 4,500 feet and above. The conditions were VFR-only for an experienced pilot, and more importantly for a pilot who knows the terrain around here like Daniel Boone knew it back in the 1700s.

Gunther and I took off for Elizabethton, maneuvering around the clouds at a low altitude mostly above and sometimes around the terrain. As we approached the Elizabethton Airport, a jet was downwind for runway six. We were headed for runway two four. I had flashbacks of my close encounter with that Citation back when I was truly a petrified and overly insecure student pilot flying one of my first solos in 4EQ.

This time I was more secure. The jet was clearly first in line to land. But more importantly, he communicated, even asked my position. We landed runway two four well after he had cleared runway six.

Gunther asked if I was ready to solo 511. I was, but decided it was best to go around with him for one more pattern just to gain confidence. While in the pattern, we decided to do a touch-and-go. Gunther was a little uptight about my execution, but I managed the maneuver well enough and came around for a stopped landing. He asked again if I was ready to solo. I said yes. I was confident. He gave me a few suggestions, took his hand-held two-way radio, and was gone. With that radio he could listen and talk to me and vice versa if I got into any trouble. He was always pushing me to extremes, but never failed to protect me from every direction. I paid no attention to his radio. I think the radio was for *his* peace of mind, sort of like a security blanket while his wife soloed her new/old airplane for the very first time.

Uneventfully, I soloed one pattern and greased the landing. *Let's try this again*, I thought. Up the taxiway I went for another pattern. *This is fun! I know what I'm doing.*

Out of nowhere a Cirrus single-engine airplane came over the radio and asked, "Can I jump ahead and take off before you? Trust me, you won't catch me."

Well, no kidding. I know your little, modern, high-tech, spitball airplane will outrun my 1969 Skylane, I thought.

But I said, "Sure, no problem. That will be fine," in a nice, friendly voice.

Spitball didn't quit annoying me. I noticed it was very noisy. I turned my head and directly behind me was that Cirrus taxiing way too close to me; his propeller almost chopping up my elevators and rudder.

I pushed my mic button and said, "It looks as if you are going to overtake me on the taxiway."

"Oh no, I'm giving you plenty of room," he says.

He was taxiing behind me like a pinball.

All I heard was Wayne's voice firmly saying "Kim, never exceed ten knots while taxiing." Remember Wayne, my FAA examiner?

I patiently maintained ten knots the entire way up the taxiway, and Spitball continued his erratic behavior while he taxied behind me.

Just prior to the runway I pulled over to the run-up area where, on two wheels, Spitball passed me, then went screeching off the runway like a rocket.

Thank goodness he's off. What a spaz!

After takeoff upon crosswind I felt the winds were picking up. It didn't bother me. I calmly and confidently continued the pattern procedures. Then I super greased that landing. *I wanna do it again.* Instead, I taxied back to the west side ramp and picked Gunther up. He got in. He was complimentary, but not overly. Why should he be? I have a pilot's license, lots of hours, and a high-performance endorsement; I *should* be soloing! I guess I was settling into being a real pilot, and he was getting used to the idea too.

I flew us back to Elk River. Winds dictated runway three zero. That's the wicked-steep descent on short final. Many pilots don't even attempt three zero. Instead they'll use runway one two if the wind and weather allows, or divert to the Elizabethton Airport. I came in focused on nailing the approach speeds. My blood was not circulating through my body at an exponential rate, my nerves were under control, and I was excited that every instrument was right on the money. The runway was exactly where it was supposed to be at each critical position.

This flying business was getting easier mentally and physically.

Four days after soloing at the Elizabethton Airport, I soloed for the very first time at Elk River on runway three zero. That was a big deal, a really big deal.

Winds were north northwest, all over the place, constantly switching 5 to 10 knots, then calm, then gusting up to 15 knots. John was right seat and I was the PIC. We did two patterns at Elk River. I did fine, but I didn't feel 100 percent confident because the winds were pushing me on downwind, and it was turbulent on the base leg. So we flew to Elizabethton to get fuel, ($5.99 a gallon—ouch! Still only $4.95 at the Ashe County Airport). The patterns and landings into Elizabethton were no problem. We talked to Dan for a few minutes while the airplane was being fueled, then we headed back to the Elk River Airport. I was hoping the winds would subside.

Nope! The winds got stronger, more erratic. Good grief. Lump in my soul. *I need to solo here—at Elk River. This is my home airport, where my airplane is hangared. Plus it's time to make it happen.*

I was anxious. *No, you're good, Kim. You can do it. You know you can,* I thought over and over again.

John and I did two more patterns on three zero. Nothing was perfect. Conditions were tough. I bounced on the landings but I had plenty of runway.

After the second pattern, John said, "Okay, let's quit, Kim."

"What? You want to quit?" I asked, stunned. *The whole purpose for this practice session is to solo at Elk River*, I thought. "NO, I don't want to quit," I said, disguising my disgust . . . I think.

He said, "Well, okay, then go solo."

"You think I can solo?" I asked.

"Yes, Kim. You can solo. Go ahead," he said calmly, maybe even a little fed up. Perhaps he rolled his eyes too and I didn't see it, as he was opening the door while the engine was still running.

"K. I'm gonna solo," I said.

I suspect he never even heard me say it. He was gone, probably thinking, *What a mental case . . . still!*

It was just me again. Alone in the airplane. I didn't like that feeling. I always had to be stern with myself—gentle, but stern. But the discouraging voice tends to get overruled nowadays. Ha.

I back taxied to runway three zero.

Again the voices were arguing back and forth with each other. *Kim, this is a tough airport. You know those winds are pushing you into the runway on downwind and base is turbulent, gusty and bumpy.*

Yeah, I know. But I just flew those same conditions four times. I did just fine and I'll do just fine this time, my calm, reasonable voice answered back.

I took off runway three zero alone. The climb out to 5,000 feet was a little bumpy, but 511 was flying strong. *Crosswind is typical; downwind I'm getting pushed. Base is bumpy and gusty. I'm a little dizzy. I'm turning a bit steeper than usual between base and final. That's okay, nothing I haven't successfully executed four times already this morning. I see the runway. Speed is fast, a little high. Push the nose down, pull the power, work the rudder pedals, carb heat, twenty degrees of flaps, long sweeping turn back to the left to get lined up with the runway. Still fast. Get it slowed down, Kim. I'm over the final mountain, about 4,200 feet, 85 mph. Full flaps, dive-bomb toward the numbers, pull the power completely, keep the airplane straight, and keep diving.*

Butterflies were trapped in my stomach just above my chest, demanding freedom. But I was holding my breath, concentrating. Trees sprinted past my window while the runway cheered my arrival. What a rush. *I got it—for sure.*

I touched down with plenty of runway to spare, bounced pretty good, added power, and baby-bounced the rest of the way down three zero.

I was shaking. That was one of those times when the demands of flying required my brain to flawlessly perform a perfectly choreographed Super Bowl halftime show. Each thought and brainwave flipped, tumbled, and maneuvered immaculately around the others while physical execution was precise. Like a symphony.

I did it.

(If anyone reading this is affiliated with the James Bond movies, this definitely qualifies me to be the next Bond girl.)

There was John, right where I'd left him, or perhaps more accurately, where he'd left me. I could tell he was proud and happy. He waved me on and followed 511 to the hangar. I shut down, secured the airplane, and exited 511.

"John, I did it, and I don't even have my purple short-sleeved shirt on!" I exclaimed.

"Great job, Kim!" he said.

"But look, here in my bag, which was in the backseat of the airplane the entire time, is my purple sweatshirt!"

He couldn't care less about my purple obsession. Landing solo on three zero at Elk River was way more impressive to John. A guy thing, I guess.

I texted Gunther, noticed my hands were still shaking, and told him I'd soloed at Elk River. It's hard to text when your hands are shaking.

He texted back, *Good job.*

Not only did I solo into Elk River on three zero, but I elicited visible excitement in my reliably calm and reserved instructor.

I couldn't wait to do it again, but better.

Of Course I Can Do It

Remember those Rosie the Riveter posters, the ones with the strong but beautiful young woman representing the American spirit during World War II? Did you know that during World War II women riveted airplanes together? Well, that's what I did, except not in a huge warehouse with zillions of other hard-working women under tough physical conditions, and I was not working on airplanes going into fierce combat. I used the same tools, did the same basic job, but in a tiny hangar tucked safely away in the Appalachian Mountains. My work was for pleasure.

511 didn't pass its static system check because one of the two static ports had a crack in it. The damaged static port is located on the nose of the pilot's side of my airplane. Gunther and I were replacing it with a good one, which meant that I had to rivet.

The static system affects the accuracy of the airspeed indicator (how fast the airplane is going—critical to staying in the air and not stalling the airplane), vertical speed indicator (measures the rate in which the airplane is climbing or descending), and the altimeter (measures how high the airplane is in the air—its altitude). Air pressure differences generated from the pitot tube and static ports operate the pitot static system. Therefore, all locations of air intake must be working properly for a pilot to rely on her/his instruments.

"Kim, this is serious work. It has to be done correctly. If you do it wrong, you could put a hole in the airplane," Gunther said unequivocally.

That's serious.

"Can you do it? Look, I have a practice area for you. Take the rivet gun, otherwise known as a pneumatic rivet hammer, place it directly over a small area of this wooden block. Don't let the gun float or wander away from the spot you chose. Pull the trigger. Do it several times till you feel you've got it. Can you do it? It has to be done correctly, no mistakes," Gunther repeated, afraid of letting me actually do it.

Since he made it sound so difficult and important, I thought, of course I can do it. All I have to do is keep a steady, firm hand. If I focus and concentrate, I can execute it. No problem.

He showed me how to properly use the rivet gun several times. I had to laugh. The noise and motion reminded me of a road construction worker using a jackhammer. That always appears to be a painful task. Barney Rubble on *The Flintstones* could never perform the job correctly. The jackhammer always got the best of him. That wouldn't happen to me.

"Gunther, what are YOU going to do?" I asked.

"One of us has to rivet outside the airplane while the other holds the bucking bar inside. Kim, maybe you should hold the bucking bar," Gunther said anxiously. "I'm very uptight about this job. Can you tell?"

"No you're not. You're fine," I said. Thinking—*If he were really insecure about this job, he wouldn't be saying so or allowing me to help.* "What do you want me to do? I'll do whatever you need," I said.

Gunther's thinking was in overdrive. He was probably wondering, *Which can she screw up the least: riveting or holding the bucking bar?*

Minutes passed. I was getting impatient.

"Make a decision, Gunther. I can do either," I said.

"Okay, you rivet. I'll get inside the airplane and hold the bucking bar." He placed one of the four rivets through a hole. "Do you see the rivet?"

"Yes, I see it," I said, excited to perform my job.

"Are you holding the gun on the rivet?" he asked impatiently.

"No, you didn't tell me to do that," I replied.

He likes it when I follow directions and has a greater appreciation when I remain patiently inactive until directions have been explicitly communicated. In the hangar, I seldom do anything unless I'm told. Leaders have a system. I understand that.

"Push the gun against the rivet and pull the trigger," he commanded.

I was sitting on that old, beat-up, rolling office chair with my latex gloves on, my face about two centimeters from 511's nose, holding the rivet gun precisely over the static port. Completely focused, I pulled the trigger timidly and began riveting. The rivet gun was loud. It's powered by an air compressor which was also loud, hence the word pneumatic. (Pneumatic means air!)

I heard yelling. I let the trigger go.

"Did you say stop?" I asked.

"Yes," Gunther yelled a little softer.

"If I'm going to hear you and we're going to do this right, you will have to yell much louder. This gun is right in my ear and it's LOUD. Be sure you yell as loud as you can. Okay?" I commanded.

"Okay. Let me see what you've done." He pulled himself out of the airplane, looked over my work and said, "Good. Good work. We have three more to go."

Each rivet I pounded better than the previous one, using the gun with more force and command. In the end, I was praised with adjectives and phrases like excellent, and that's professional work.

I was not just a helper anymore. I was leaps and bounds from being an aeronautical engineer, but I was becoming a skilled airplane mechanic's . . . assistant.

Back at home, Olivia wanted to make strawberry ice cream and was waiting for me to pick up a few ingredients at the store before she could get started. Off I went, back to being a mom!

CHAPTER SEVEN
The Cutest Thing

I needed to practice and perfect flying in controlled airspace. Most of my flying as a student was done in uncontrolled airspace, in and out of airports with no traffic controller. The actual flying within the controlled airspace was not my problem. Having knowledge of, understanding, and conforming to the air traffic controller's verbal commands and knowing which controller to speak to on a particular frequency was my problem. Controlled and uncontrolled airports are laid out throughout the United States. It's valuable, not to mention required by the FAA, to be familiar with procedures for every type of airport and airspace.

"Gunther, I need you to help me fly in and out of the Tri-Cities Airport."

The last time we had done this it was sort of a disaster. He had been impatient, and he ended up doing all the communicating with the traffic controllers, while I did all the flying. I'm sure my behavior somehow encouraged his impatience.

"Okay, but let's be prepared this time," he said. "You and I need to go through a potential conversation between a pilot and air traffic control, and it would help if you listen to liveatc.net periodically."

"Okay, great ideas. Walk me through a flight scenario into Tri-Cities, and I'll write it down," I said.

There I went, having to write everything down again. I'm

not afraid to do whatever works for me; I don't care if people think I'm slow, weird, unconventional, or even stupid. It's my life, and since I'm still scared in the air, I'm going to overprepare. It takes some of my fear away.

Gunther started explaining the procedures rapidly.

"Wait, wait, wait. I can't write that fast. Please slow down," I said. He did.

Here's what I wrote down, and what I would actually take with me the next time I flew to Tri-Cities, with the exception of the parenthetical definitions. Keep in mind that in addition to getting the communication jargon down, I still had to fly the airplane.

- About twenty miles prior to landing, listen to ATIS—118.25. (ATIS (automated terminal information system) is a continuous broadcast of recorded airport/terminal area and weather information. The broadcast contains essential information, such as weather information, active runways, available approaches, and any other information helpful to the pilot.)
- Contact Tri-Cities approach on 134.42.
- "Tri-Cities approach Skylane 71511 over."
- "Skylane 71511 go ahead."
- "Tri-Cities approach Skylane 71511 is ten miles to the southeast with information 'Bravo' landing Tri-Cities." (The ATIS report assigns a letter designation (e.g. "b" for bravo) from the International Civil Aviation Organization spelling alphabet to each new report. The letter progresses down the alphabet with every update and starts at alpha after a break in service of twelve hours or more. This allows air traffic controllers to verify whether the pilot has the current information.)
- "71511 squawk 0141 expect runway two three." (There are

four available runways in Tri-Cities. ATIS lets me know which one is active.)

- "Tri-Cities approach Skylane 71511 squawk 0141 expecting runway two three OR report the runway in sight."
- Pre-landing checklist.
- "71511 contact tower 119.5."
- "Tri-Cities approach Skylane 71511 contact tower 119.5."
- Dial in 119.5
- "Tri-Cities tower Skylane 71511 with you."
- "Hey Kim, this is Ed, where's Gunther?"

Just kidding, Gunther and I both know Ed. He's a traffic controller. Really nice guy. Sometimes he breaks routine and chats briefly. That's what neighborly, familiar airport controllers are like: friendly and personable. They automatically help out when you're a petrified, insecure student.

- "Skylane 71511 cleared to land runway two three."
- "Skylane 71511 roger cleared to land runway two three."
- LAND!
- Turn off first available taxiway. Wait on taxiway. Do not move until instructed by traffic controller.
- "Skylane 71511 right turn on yankee, contact ground 121.7." OR "Skylane 71511 right turn on yankee, right turn on alpha, cross runway niner to the ramp, stay with this frequency."
- "Tri-Cities ground Skylane 71511 clear of the runway would like to taxi to runway two three and depart to NC06 at 5,500 feet."
- "71511 are you ready to copy your departure instructions?" (Or controller will just give me instructions.)
- "71511 departure frequency is 134.42, squawk 0417, after

departure fly 180, climb to @ or below 3,500 feet."

- "Skylane 71511 departure frequency is 134.42, squawk 0417, after departure fly 180, climb to @ or below 3,500 feet."
- Enter the squawk, go to the end of the taxiway and hold the line.
- When I'm ready I call the tower 119.5.
- "Tri-Cities tower Skylane 71511 ready to go runway two three."
- (Three possible instructions.)
    - "71511 hold short."
    - "71511 line up and wait."
    - "71511 cleared for takeoff runway two three."
- "Tri-Cities tower, Skylane 71511 cleared for takeoff runway two three."
- "Skylane 71511 cleared for takeoff runway two three."
- TAKE OFF (follow departure instructions).
- At some point after takeoff, tower will tell me to contact departure at 134.42.
- Dial in departure frequency 134.42.
- "Tri-Cities departure Skylane 71511 climbing to 3,500 feet, turning 180."
- "71511 climb to requested altitude, direct destination."
- "Skylane 71511 roger climbing to 5,500 feet heading 134."
- Fly along to my heading and altitude. Heading of 134 degrees from Tri-Cities to Elk River.
- "Tri-Cities departure Skylane 71511 I would like to cancel flight following."
- "71511 flight following cancelled, squawk VFR (1200), good day."
- "511 roger, thank you."

It's Not Because I'm A Girl

When I flew commercial or with Gunther, it never occurred

to me that the pilots might be anything but confident. Not in a million years would I have thought that they could experience anxiety or have butterflies in their stomachs. But they do and seldom let you know . . . until in casual, trusting conversation they admit it.

Gunther has mentioned his fears several times, and John even admitted he was scared once. But I thought they were just saying that to encourage me. I didn't really take them seriously.

I was peeling the door seals off 511, another maintenance project, when our friend Stuart popped by the Elk River Airport hangar. His hangar is next to ours where the Cheyenne is kept. Pilots just like to stop by and chat for hours.

Stuart showed Gunther and me his pretty much brand-new, glass-cockpit, all-leather interior (even the yokes) Beechcraft Bonanza. It even has air conditioning and heat. Beautiful!!! 511 doesn't have AC, a glass cockpit, or a leather interior. Neither does 4 Echo Quebec.

The conversation evolved to his flying, or lack thereof.

"Stuart, why don't you fly more often?" I asked, amazed since he had that exceptionally beautiful Bonanza and seemingly lots of time.

"I just don't feel comfortable flying in and out of Elk River. What if an engine fails? The turbulence is rough here. I don't like turbulence," he freely admitted.

"You need to do what I do: practice as much as you can. Get an instructor, or better yet, grab Gunther and do laps over and over again right here at Elk River," I said, as if it was a no-brainer.

He agreed and mentioned that he had practiced and still felt insecure. But more importantly, he admitted his fears to a beginner, female pilot. When Stuart, who is an IFR-rated pilot, told me he worries, it hit me! I realized I experience fear and anxiety not because I'm a girl and new at this, but because I'm human. Gender and experience don't matter. I'm a pilot now, part of the club.

Family and Friends

My brother Erich flew with me for the first time. I took him to
Elizabethton and back. He appeared unruffled and completely
at ease, with not a worry in the world. I was nervous, as usual,
mainly about the landings. As we passed over Watauga Lake,
Erich asked if we could fly lower, closer to the lake. The lakes
here are unique, beautiful of course, surrounded by lush, mostly
deciduous tree-covered mountains that climb straight out of the
water to 4,500 feet or so. They tuck me in and make me feel safe.

Erich loves the lake and wakeboarding. He has a boat and
goes to Watauga Lake with his family and friends every chance
he gets. I would have loved to accommodate his request. We
could've done the Bond thing, even flown under the Butler
Bridge, which a handful of pilots have done. (I won't name any
names.) But I nervously said, "No, Erich, I have to stick to my
plan and the route that I've practiced. I don't dare veer off course
or violate any VFR rules." He knows that about me, that I'm a
rule follower, 99 percent of the time. And usually the other 1
percent is Krista's fault. He knows that, too.

Erich and I headed home to Elk River. I landed fine.

"I'll fly with you anytime," Erich said.

A few hours later, I got a text with several pictures of Erich
and me flying. The caption said, *Flying with my big sister.*

While flying with Erich and after clearing runway two four
in Elizabethton, Fulton came over the radio and said "Hi, how's
the bird flying?"

Fulton's an older gentleman, semiretired, and usually only
works on Sundays and Mondays at the airport. Last summer he
asked his wife if he could dip into their retirement account so he
could buy an old-fashioned, single-seat, open-cockpit airplane.

It's a home-built low-wing monoplane made of wood and fabric, incredibly light. It's called a Fly Baby—a modest airplane! *La Petite Oiseau Rouge.* It means "little lady red bird." French, obviously. That's how Fulton refers to his Fly Baby. Affectionately named after his mom and wife. His little lady holds twelve gallons of fuel, and has a range of 2.5 hours, which can take you about 115 miles in optimal weather conditions. It'll cruise at 75 to 80 mph. Its empty weight is 690 pounds, but with full fuel and luggage it can handle 925 pounds.

He showed it to me one day, and even let me sit in it. You know when Snoopy flies his airplane? That's how I felt when I sat in Fulton's Fly Baby. I imagined the wind blowing through my hair under my unstrapped leather helmet, bugs pelting my oversized black goggles, the air hugging my body while my scarf waved behind my shoulders. I firmly, with two hands, held the control stick located between my legs. The control stick acts like the yoke, controlling the ailerons and elevators. My feet rested on the rudder pedals and brakes. I scanned the instruments on the miniature panel and pretended to fly Fulton's vintage aircraft.

The instrument panel has so few gauges I got confused. (Only a blonde can say that and get away with it, right?) Directly in front of me was the airspeed indicator. Fulton mentioned that it doesn't really work.

"What? You need that," I said.

"No you don't. I just feel the airplane. She tells me how she's doing," he said.

"Ookaay. I'll go with that," I said unconvincingly with my eyeballs rolled to the upper left hand corners of my sockets.

At the very top from left to right on the instrument panel, Fly Baby has an altimeter, a vertical speed indicator, an oil pressure and oil temperature gauge, a magneto switch, an engine rpm gauge and a clock—the only digital instrument in the airplane. Randomly situated is a compass, which cost him $20 on Amazon. It was certified, he assured me.

From left to right on the bottom of the instrument panel

is the throttle, carburetor heat knob, primer knob, slip/skid indicator and a fuel control valve on/off knob. That's it; no gyroscopic instruments driven by electricity or a vacuum, like an attitude indicator or a directional gyro (DG). Not even navigation or communication instruments like a GPS or a VOR. He does have a hand held VHF communication radio and headset. The control stick has the push-to-talk button.

There's no heat, no roof, no doors, no amp meter (because there's no electrical system), no lights and no suction gauge ('cause there's no vacuum pump). No traditional fuel gauge either. But, beyond the windshield, dead center on the nose is a bobbing wire attached to a cork that plunges into the tank and floats on the surface of the fuel. When the long wire protruding from the nose of the airplane isn't visible, it's time to consider getting some fuel.

The master turn buckle, which holds the wings together (literally, it holds the wings together!), is located below the instrument panel. It was a puzzling mystery to me. So much so that I ignored it. Honestly, it intimidated me. It was one of those situations when ignorance is bliss. But Fulton insisted that I learn more than I wished to know. The visibly indispensable, heavy, and sturdy metal rod tightens or loosens the wing wires. If the turn buckle fails, the wings collapse and you're doomed.

Turn buckle aside, I was excited and thought about asking Fulton if he would take me flying. Before I asked that dumb question, I realized the airplane is a single-seater. Duh!

When I was a student pilot I saw Fulton randomly, every now and then at the airport in passing. He always cleaned 4 Echo Quebec's windshield. My first flight by myself after I soloed, Fulton came up to me just before I started the airplane and said, "Congratulations on soloing."

I was part of the club.

Show-Off

I took Gunther and my typed list for entering and exiting controlled airspace and practiced flying into Tri-Cities once again. My list helped, but I still needed practice.

We did two laps. My flying was fine, but the communications part was less than par. I continued to stumble and get caught unprepared when the controllers spoke or when I had to respond. Repetition was key for me. Gunther said I could do it by myself. But I didn't feel I could. Not yet.

The first lap over, Gunther and I got along just fine. Second lap—well . . . he was mean to me. Okay, I'm probably exaggerating. Let's put it this way: we didn't agree.

Gunther tightened the parameters of the rules. The departure controller said "71511, after departure climb and maintain at or below 3,500 feet, fly 180 degrees." Well, after takeoff, I didn't immediately turn 180 degrees. I wanted to fly the runway heading until I had reached 2,000 feet. That altitude guaranteed I would clear any ground obstacles. Then I would turn to the 180-degree heading.

Shortly after we were off the ground, Gunther said sternly, "The controller said to fly a heading of 180 degrees."

"I will, but I'm going to reach 2,000 feet before I make any kind of a turn. John and Wayne both taught me that," I replied, annoyed.

"Kim, there's an airliner ready to depart once you're clear," Gunther snapped, irritated by my disobedience.

"I don't care about that airliner right now. It's more important for me to fly safely before I consider accommodating anyone else on the ground," I snapped back.

And what makes that airliner any more important than me? I thought.

Silence.

I knew he was upset with me. I didn't care. I was the pilot-in-command, and my performance was well within the parameters of safe flying. Gunther's parameters were just a little tighter than mine. He flies a Cheyenne, which has a whole lot more power than my Skylane. He can climb fast and reach a safe maneuvering altitude much quicker than I can. I was sticking with what I'd learned.

The argument didn't end. "I'm never flying with you again. I come out here to help you, and all you do is yell at me," Gunther said.

Now he was exaggerating. I didn't yell.

I knew he'd fly with me again. It was an empty threat, but one I had to respect at that moment.

I kept quiet. Actions speak louder than words. I'd show him.

My approach and landing on runway one two into Elk River were perfect.

"Show-off!" was all he said after I landed.

Clearly, still, I had issues with controlled airspace. Nevertheless I rustled up enough courage to attempt to venture from the Elk River Airport to the Tri-Cities Airport on my own. The skies were crystal clear and the air was calm at my elevation and above. However, the Tri-Cities Airport reported a low ceiling: 500 feet. Local pilots (I'm a local pilot now) know that it's fog from the nearby Boone Lake and it typically burns off quickly. I got in the air and saw that it wasn't the typical Boone Lake fog. Clouds hovered thick and low against most every valley floor as if sleeping blankets hadn't been lifted for the day ahead.

"I'm not going to Tri-Cities. Clouds are between you and the runway, and you can't fly through clouds," I said.

I still do talk to myself out loud when I fly alone.

"Okay, plan B. Elizabethton is perfect. No cloud cover.

Let's go there," I continued.

I had my GPS and frequencies set for Tri-Cities. They needed to be reset to the Elizabethton Airport. My blue folder containing critical flight information for Elk River and Elizabethton flew with me everywhere. I glanced over to the copilot's seat, which was occupied by my iPad and blue folder, so that I could recall the frequencies for Elizabethton. I dialed in the frequencies, flew the pattern for runway six, and landed with ease at the Elizabethton Airport. Immediately I took off and headed back home.

The flight was pleasant and I was confident, even when the guys on the Elk River Unicom said "Kim [they call me Kim, not 511], those geese are on the runway again. We'll send security down there to shoo them away."

"Elk River Unicom, Skylane 71511, Okay, I'm on a three-mile final," I said.

"Kim, Bill's got the geese taken care of," Carter reported.

"Okay, 511 roger. Thank you, thank you very much." I was relieved, but knew they'd get it taken care of.

But while I was landing on runway one two, inches from touchdown, not more than 100 feet in front of me, that pesky flock of geese crossed my flight path at an angle. I wasn't worried, though. The geese had their space. I had mine. Life moved on safely . . . for all of us.

Before I knew it, flying in the controlled airspace in and around the Tri-Cities Airport would be routine. It would simply take a few more attempts and plenty of courage.

From my kitchen window I can see far, far to the West, well into Tennessee and Virginia. The weather looked good; the sky was Carolina blue, zero wind. But . . . the forecast was for mostly cloudy.

Clear, calm, no wind persisted, so I headed to the Elk River Airport, performed a preflight inspection, reviewed my checklists, started up the Skylane, and took off from runway three zero for a practice run to the Elizabethton Airport. I didn't have anyone to fly with me, so I was not venturing into Tri-Cities airspace only to be spooked again by the weather. Tri-Cities would have to wait.

As soon as I took off, I noticed the clouds were moving quickly from the east. I kept turning my head backward to see the cloud cover behind me. It was rolling seamlessly over the mountains. I leveled out at 4,500 feet, reduced power, closed the cowl flaps, adjusted the prop, and listened to Elizabethton AWOS. Wind was 09 at 3. That means landing on runway six. I turned my head again to see what the weather was doing behind me.

"I need to turn back if I want to get home," I said to myself, nervously.

If I can't see because of weather, I can't fly back home.

I changed the GPS back to NC06, the identifier for Elk River, and gently turned the yoke to the left. I changed my communication frequency back to Elk River and adjusted the rudder. I couldn't see beyond Three-Mile Hill. I was getting uptight.

"I can get under the clouds. No, I can't see beyond Three-Mile Hill even if I can get under the clouds. The mountains are obscured. I'm not doing it," I said both confidently and insecurely —if you can be both at the same time!

I zigzagged a bit to see from varying angles. I couldn't see enough.

"I'm not doing it." Confirmed.

I changed the GPS again, turned back to Elizabethton, and landed there. I was surprised that I had kept cool and successfully managed to change the GPS three times in the air without messing it up . . . and managed to fly the airplane at the same time.

Safely on the ground at 0A9 (Elizabethton) I decided to

take off and fly a pattern. That way I could see what the weather was doing to the east. It was bumpy up there. The airplane was getting ahead of me, and I was feeling awkwardly insecure.

"I'm getting back on the ground and staying there," I said.

After shut down at the Elizabethton Airport, I called Gunther who said, "Where are you?"

"I'm in Elizabethton," I replied.

"You're crazy. What are you going to do?" he asked.

"I'm going to ask Dan if I can borrow the crew car and drive home," I said.

I drove home.

A few days later Gunther and I had flown to Ashe County (KGEV) to fill up 511. One hundred low lead was $5.05, still the cheapest around. The runway was uphill when landing on two eight; eighty feet difference from one end to the other. As I approached closer and closer, I felt like I was playing a video game. The uphill slope created a disorienting appearance. The surrounding terrain and upper end of the runway were closing in on me, while the runway numbers were falling away. My eyes intuitively focused on the opposite end of the runway and blocked out the illusions. That helped, and kept my mind focused and solid. I touched down nicely.

The cutest thing happened that day. Upon arrival at the Ashe County Airport, I was pleasantly greeted by the two local women's clubs. As we taxied onto the ramp, Gunther noticed a large group of ladies lined up in front of the terminal building taking pictures: of us! I parked the Skylane, got out, and politely said to Eric, the nice employee, to fill her up. I gathered up my belongings, draped my tote bag over my shoulder and headed for the terminal. The ladies were still there. They didn't budge, and kept pleasantly looking at me. I walked closer and was intimidated—I didn't know what to do or how to behave. They were standing right in front of the terminal door. There were eleven of 'em.

Do I keep going?

I couldn't. They were a barrier, blocking my entry into the terminal building.

Sweetly, they held their position.

"Hi Ladies! Whatcha doing?" I asked.

Boy, they didn't stop talking. They huddled around me closer and closer, each one bombarding me with question after question. "What kind of an airplane is that?" "Where are you from?" "Wow, you're a pilot? When did you learn to fly?" "Is it hard? That looks like Ronnie Ray's old airplane—is it? Did you know Ronnie Ray flew that airplane to the Bahamas?" and so on. I felt like the new kid in the play yard. It was really special. I eagerly answered each one of them. But, I was more interested in being the inquisitor. I wanted to know about them. When it became appropriate, I squeezed in my questions, lots of them.

"Who are you ladies, and why are you hanging out at the airport?" were just two of my questions.

The president of one of the clubs was the main spokeswoman. But the president of the other club chimed in every now and then.

"We do lots of things. We work with the heart group, the blood drives, help elderly people. We perform eye and ear tests on schoolchildren and make quilts and afghans for those in need. Today we're here touring the airport."

"Ooooh, so you ladies do a lot of volunteer work?" I stated and asked at the same time.

One of the members, not a president, wasn't shy about replying, "Yeah, but we get together for meals and parties, too."

"You know, I make really good chocolate chip cookies," I said.

"Well, then, you can come to our next meeting. It's on November sixth," the candid member replied.

Another member added, "We'll take cookies or a covered dish, just bring something."

In between the fun and interesting exchanges, I invited them to see my airplane.

"Oooh, yes, we'd love to look inside," many said in unison.

Like a herd of clucking hens, we all walked over to my airplane. They peeked inside, in awe, impressed.

One lady inspected the instrument panel and said, "Wow, I'd take my hat off to you if I had a hat on."

Cute, I thought! *Classically old-fashioned, polite.*

We shimmied back toward the terminal and gabbed some more. All the while Gunther busied himself with Eric, helping to fuel my airplane. I don't think Gunther wanted to get involved with me and the ladies. Plus, I told the gals that he was my mechanic. Eventually word got out that he was my husband!

"Kim, let's go," Gunther said.

"Okay, okay," I replied.

"Ladies, I need to get inside to pay for my fuel," I said.

They backed up, creating a red carpet walkway like at the Oscars so I could enter the terminal. They followed me inside, and then headed for their meeting room.

I loved talking with them.

I detoured to the counter to pay my bill and chatted with Eric.

"Kim, are you leaving?" a lady asked.

"Yes, I'm heading back home," I replied.

She hollered to her group, who were taking seats in the lecture room, "Ladies, ladies, come back, Kim's taking off. Let's watch her."

They quickly and energetically walked back outside.

Before Gunther and I loaded into my Skylane, the ladies wanted a picture of us. And that's after they had already taken several group pictures with just me. We posed nicely for them.

Focusing so as not to get distracted by my new lady friends, I carefully read over my checklists and then started the Skylane. With lots of energy, I waved good-bye to the ladies. They ALL waved back. I taxied to runway one zero and took off. I knew they would watch me until I was a tiny, red speck on the horizon.

I think I'm gonna run for president . . . of the United States. I'll load up my little red airplane, fly around the country with my mechanic (that's Gunther) right seat, invite all of the men's and ladies' clubs to each small-town airport, and just listen.

I did it, I did it! Yes. I flew to the Tri-Cities Airport and back—all by myself. You knew I could do it, didn't you?

The weather was perfect. Nothing to worry about there. I had butterflies in my stomach and the adrenaline was pumping—not out of control though. For the most part, all went smoothly, just as I had practiced over and over since July.

After arriving safely back at Elk River, I properly shut down the Skylane. No wait, that's not true: I accidentally flipped the master switch off before the engine actually quit. Oops. I meant to turn off the master avionics switch, which is right next to the master. But it didn't seem to bother anything. No piercing sounds or smoke from the engine, no vibrations or oddities. I flicked the master back on, pretending it had never happened, and continued to follow the shutdown checklist.

Remember when I got my private pilot's license and I was so excited that all I wanted to do was throw my arms in the air and jump around hootin' and hollerin' like a crazed lunatic at the gas station off I-81 or whatever highway that was in Virginia or Tennessee, but I never did? I got lost instead. Well, when I finally went in and out of Tri-Cities (controlled airspace) all by myself for the very first time, I behaved like a crazed lunatic.

No one saw me.

I got out of my Skylane, threw my arms in the air and jumped up and down, hootin' and hollerin'. I jumped up and down again, because it was fun and felt really good. Then I got my camera, programmed the self-timer, set it on the trash can (which I rolled out of my hangar), and captured several pictures of me jumping in the air in front of 511 *again.*

I don't think anyone saw me try to put my airplane in the hangar that day either. At least I hope not. Using the 1969 Skylane-issued skinny, red tow bar, I always manually pull 511 from the hangar and push it back in when I'm finished. It isn't easy. But Gunther thinks I'm plenty strong enough to manage that powerful task without any sort of fuel-driven, motorized assistance. I wasn't going to argue with him.

That time, though, I couldn't get 511 in the hangar. I didn't have the strength. Perhaps all the jumping up and down had worn me out! I began to push and steer 511 into its hangar. It rolled back out before it reached the doorway. Good grief! I pulled it back out, pushed wicked hard, and began running to ensure enough momentum to get the Skylane over the baby hump just outside the hangar door's entry edge. 511 then cleared the hump. Thank goodness. But I lost control of the steering. *Oh, crap, this'll surely be the end of me if I smash a wing into the hangar.* I regained control, pushed my helpless airplane safely to its resting place, and stood for several minutes, recuperating. My heart was thumping out of my chest from exertion. I mentally slowed my heart rate to about 70 beats per minute and eventually caught my breath. Exhausted, I lazily closed the hangar door, secured the latches, switched the lights off, locked the side door and walked to my car. I sat for a while, dizzy. To safeguard against passing out, I texted. My heart was definitely strained. Maybe I should go buy a motorized tug.

100 Percent Confidence

Floyd is eighty-nine years old. He'll be ninety in May. He grew up among the coal mines of Pennsylvania. His hard work and the GI bill put him through college. He's a retired doctor now. Close to seventy years ago, he flew bombing missions in World War II as an officer in the Air Corps. I took him up flying today. He was right seat. A girl half his age was left seat and the pilot-in-command. Imagine how the world has changed over his lifetime.

Floyd's no ordinary (almost) nonagenarian. As a matter of fact, most of the old-guy friends I inherited from Gunther are remarkable. They debate heartily with me, never cut me any slack, sometimes even agree with me, often talk over each other, treat me with respect and chivalry (which I appreciate). They teach me things about the past, the present, and the future that I am eager to add to my database of knowledge. Old folks, they're raising the bar and setting higher standards for human longevity. I wanna be like them when I grow older.

Floyd and I took off after I diligently went through all of my checklists and run-up. I walked him through my routine to be polite and because talking out loud still provides an extra bit of security.

"Are you nervous, Floyd?" I asked once we leveled out and reached cruising altitude.

"No Kim, I have 100 percent confidence in you," he said with a smile and more assurance than I think I've ever had in myself.

A wave of pride traveled through me. I smiled back.

We talked a bit throughout the flight, but not much. During our attentive silence, I wondered if he was thinking back to the days when he was a young man, barely twenty years old, flying bombers in Europe. I didn't dare ask, but that's the impression I inferred. He seemed miles away, reliving a time I'll never understand. I couldn't begin to comprehend the fear, maturity, and composure of guys like him.

Our flight was uneventful in terms of weather or me having an internal, emotional meltdown. We landed at the Elizabethton Airport and immediately took off for Virginia Highlands, landed there and took off again. I needed fuel, so we ventured back over South Holston Lake, Shady Valley, Cross Mountain, and back into Elizabethton. Once the guys fueled 511, we headed back to Elk River and landed.

"Floyd, can you help me push the airplane into the hangar?" I politely asked.

"Sure. Where do you want me to push?" he responded.

"Right there on the strut," I said.

As we pushed the Skylane into the hangar I thought, *Kim. He's almost ninety years old, a skinny little guy, and you're having him push a 3,000-pound airplane. What are you thinking?*

Right on cue, my calm, reasonable voice answered back, *He can do it.*

Afterword

It's been nearly two years since I earned my private pilot's license. Ease and confidence in controlled airspace is still a work in progress. I'm no longer deathly afraid to fly in small airplanes, but I do maintain a healthy dose of fear. I fly alone with greater mental ease and feel comfortable when bringing passengers along. I know a great deal more about engines and oil than before, but most importantly, when I fly I realize we're all part of a community, a place in the sky that temporarily takes us into a world that exists high above the earth and away from the general human population, its stereotypes and prejudices. Pilots and traffic controllers: that's all the club allows. We're all different: men, women, varying social status, ugly, pretty, atheists, believers, agnostics, politically motivated, apolitical, friendly, grouchy, shy, bold, egotistical, reserved, respectful, rude, high school students, Ph Ds, young, middle-aged, old, very old, scared, confident, and everything in between.

Each characteristic exists up there in the sky, far from the hustle and bustle of society and all of its demands and idiosyncrasies. But in the air, we all get along and play by the same rules. The variables don't change because of who we are or who we're not, and they certainly don't change with what we have or what we don't have. If the lines are ever crossed, none of us get away with it, and rightfully so. We all take care of each other up there.

And then, eventually, we land.

Acknowledgments

Learning to fly took guts and courage—and a few people who believed in me. Gunther believes I can do just about anything. With that kind of faith, oftentimes I'm nutty enough to think he's right. This time he was. Steadfastly, he supported me every step of the way.

John Barker's patience, respect, and dedication turned a student like me into a pilot. Not an easy task.

Krista was always there when I needed a texting companion or a hand to hold me up.

John Carter is the craziest and loudest person I know. He thought my flying story was worth publishing, and was the one who led me to my editor, Betsy Thorpe, who led me to my copy editor, Maya Packard, and my designer, Diana Wade. Without Betsy and Maya's guidance, this book wouldn't be. I am amazed with their expertise and infinite attention to detail. They just get it. Diana beautifully designed the book and captured the cover I was after.

I am grateful to a handful of friends who took the time to read my stories, chapter by chapter, in their unedited, raw forms. Even at that stage, they encouraged me. You know who you are.

Olivia, my little star, tells it like it is. She keeps me grounded, and she and Gunther remind me every day that love is unequivocal.

Sherri and Erich were among the first to bravely fly with me. Thanks for trusting me.

Lastly, but most importantly, the core of who I am is a gift from my parents, and that won't change. I'm a lucky girl.

CPSIA information can be obtained
at www.ICGtesting.com
Printed in the USA
FSOW02n2144120117
29598FS

9 780997 150704